EMILY'S ROBERT E.

T-M Fitzgerald

PublishAmerica
Baltimore

Hardcover 978-1-4626-0883-6
Softcover 978-1-4626-0882-9
PUBLISHED BY PUBLISHAMERICA, LLLP
www.publishamerica.com
Baltimore

Printed in the United States of America

DEDICATION

On March 19, 2003 former United States President George W. Bush declared war on the little West-Asian country of Iraq. On August 31, 2010 after 2,721 days, succeeding President, Barack Obama declared the mission officially over. Sure, on paper the operation/war was over, but what about who and what was left behind?

This book is dedicated to all people on all sides of war and is meant to remind the public at large how we should continue to remember; not only those lost to the occupation of Iraq, but just as importantly, all those left behind; on both sides. This book is for all family members who, at whatever moment in time it was, whatever side they were on, never had to be asked, "Are you..."- this book is dedicated to all of those who already knew.

ACKNOWLEDGEMENTS

Among those I wish to acknowledge and thank for making this project possible are a number of people (both living and deceased) whose quotes, articles and books gave me tremendous insight on the subject of human nature. I wish to thank Marc Grossman, Tennessee Williams, Sybil Leek, E.F. Tripp, David L. Phillips, Riverbend, Robert Meskin, Michael A. Phillips, Todd S. Purdum, James Brady, Peter W. Galbraith, Michael V. Uschan, Lucy Danziger and Catherine Burndorf, Larry Smith, D. Miller, G. Mitchell, K. Holmstedt, James Jones, and A. Swofford. I also wish to thank Briona L. Chambers, USMC and extend extremely heartfelt and most profound thanks to Mr. David Simon of Southbend, Indiana. Thank you former Army Warrant Officer/Viet Nam veteran William Marshall Fitzgerald, Sr. for going above and beyond and to J.L. Fitzgerald, fellow veteran for your valuable insight and encouragement. Also, for giving me the brilliant flashes of inspiration which helped me create several key portions of this story, I wish to thank my friend from Fairbanks, Alaska Mr. Kevin Thompson, who was one of about half a dozen people who critically analyzed my final draft. I also thank James Kellogg, former classmate/fellow veteran, who unselfishly shared his experiences with me from when he served active duty in Iraq. Last but certainly not least, I also wish to thank Mr. J.R. Cash and JD Laudermilk…

"Bad news travels like wildfire. Good news travels real slow."

INTRODUCTION

Some years back, while making our way due south one Easter holiday, my son and I found ourselves meandering across some of the flattest country we'd ever wandered. That particular weekend found us traveling south east across the vast delta of the Mississippi River in no particular hurry to get anywhere, simply taking in the variety of sites along the way. Of course, playing in the background, keeping perfect time with the rhythm of every bump on the road was one of my ever-present Johnny Cash CD's.

As the opening strains of The Ballad of Ira Hayes met our ears, I found my eyes focusing on what appeared to be an extremely aged cemetery located in the middle of that endless delta. While Johnny Cash serenaded us, I found myself making way to the cemetery's entrance, for no other reason than curiosity's and verify just how old the cemetery truly was.

We slowly eased onto the lane leading into the cemetery, which was little more than a rutted, dirt path with grass growing in the middle of it. As I rolled down my window to get a better look, I found my eyes scrolling headstones in various stages of disrepair. I quickly determined it wasn't as old of a cemetery as I'd first believed, just a sadly neglected one. I found myself wondering where all these peoples' family members had gone which further fueled the creative wheels of imagination already spinning in my mind. Why hadn't anybody been by for at least that first obligatory spring-mowing of the grass? What happened to all the people these folks had left behind? Of course, listening to Ira Hayes lent me to begin thinking very specifically about veterans in particular that were inevitably buried there and wondering about the different wars and conflicts in American history they'd been a part of. This made me think about the war of my generation; Iraq post 911 and all the dead buried because of it. An endless chain reaction started going off in my mind about so many things, all because I ventured to stop at that old cemetery.

No longer was enlisting in the military simply a way to pay for college or for gaining a practical life skill. The war in Iraq gave Americans new vocabulary to digest. Words like impasse, insurgency, Taliban and Al Quaeda were just a few terms that quickly became familiar fare on a daily basis. Despite the fact that expressions like air-strikes, road-side bombings, and martyrdom were also becoming regular media fodder, one word in particular became increasingly frequent but almost casually overlooked; casualties.

In the beginning, reports about Iraqi casualties were almost non-existent and figures concerning American casualties? Well, it seemed nobody was allowed to know anything for sure about those particular numbers. Apparently, out of sight meant out of mind as well. Just like when the declaration of war was officially made, it didn't seem such a big deal to most people.

"Another war in Iraq? The first one only lasted how long?"

All too soon in cities and towns across America, the names of soldiers killed in Iraq started showing up in local papers. Those names weren't always from the next town over, either.

"Hey, my kid graduated with that guy."

"My daughter dated that boy."

"That's my nephew."

Names turned familiar and war over there became personal over here. Soldiers weren't just getting deployed/called to duty; they were dying, a fact that increasingly impressed itself upon our minds; at least until the television was turned off or the newspaper tossed into the recycle bin. People at home too quickly ceased being affected by what has been called, among other things, 'The Occupation of Iraq'.

To many Americans, the media's nonstop coverage of events in Iraq was merely sensationalizing some latest statistic to improve network ratings or was an attempt by the government to rally public support for our nation's continued participation in the war. 'Just breaking' news bulletins were about events taking place thousands of miles away in a little piss-ant country hardly anybody had ever heard about; a place very few cared about. Not many Americans knew any details about the little country nestled in a desert on the other side of the world other than it being some place situated thousands of miles away from the relative sanctity of their homes in towns all along America's fertile hills and rolling plains.

War in Iraq apparently wasn't supposed to be real like World War II. No, that kind of war didn't happen anymore. And Viet Nam was how long ago? Da Nang and Saigon? Who cares what happened in Bosnia? When it came to Iraq, it could be debated that the American public had too quickly reached the point of over-saturation.

Numerous books suddenly popped up, written in pro or con sentiment, opinions were unashamedly expressed for the world to read. Movies were eventually produced, and television networks started turning over shows attempting to give everybody 'back home' accurate portrayal of the way life was for our soldiers 'over there' and for their spouses 'over here.' It was quite on purpose we did not see pictures or comprehensive news coverage of our soldiers when they were brought home via Dover Airbase, Delaware in their flag-draped coffins. Bodies of our fallen military were flown home in the dead of night so nobody could see the 'dignified transport of remains'. News footage regarding such was strictly regulated if not outright forbidden. The press wasn't allowed to see or report on our casualties so people conveniently never recognized the impact that the Iraqi war was having…until aspects of what was happening over there hit closer to home.

As far as America knew, the war in Iraq a la 2003 was simply going to be little more than another one of those 'shows of force'. We'd get over there, get whatever we had to do to get done, get out and all the little soldiers would return home safely. A few months later, we would gather together and watch a recap on the six o'clock news. That, as we now know, was certainly not the case.

It wasn't long before we started to hear about or watch stories of war protesters showing up at military funerals. Protesters at military funerals? Nobody was broadcasting reports about American casualties, so how many funerals could they possibly be talking about or protesting? On the six o'clock news, we learned about Patriot Riders; individuals unfurling purposefully positioned American flags at cemeteries to shield fallen veteran's families from those protesters. It was only then that America started to consider how maybe this time, war 'over there' wasn't what we were being so conditioned to accept. It was different this time and simply blasting through the cold, hard facts wasn't going to do.

Books, songs, articles, and movies about other wars, other people, were created long before the business in Iraq. As a matter of fact, remember Ira Hayes? He was a real person, a Pima Indian from Arizona. (Recall the Joe Rosenthal photograph of a certain flag-raising on Mount Suribachi, Iwo Jima? Ira was one of the Marines on the mount.) War was not something new, something unheard of. But if it was so important that Americans fought for their country, if it were such a big deal when we conquered our enemy in whatever our endeavor was at the moment, why weren't Americans allowed to witness, much less honor the dead coming back home? Why was there such effort put into controlling the images that the American public could see about this war in the first place?

Interestingly enough, only a small percentage of Americans can claim the status of Veteran. Though current statistics weren't available, in 2008, that figure was less than ten percent. It's been because of an all-volunteer force that America remains what it is today; free and safe. (Relatively speaking, of course.) We must always remember the individuals who chose to wear the uniforms of America's armed forces, no matter what our personal feelings may be. When we consciously choose to turn off the television or change the radio station citing those casualty reports, we choose to forget about that ten percent who chose to keep America safe.

As with the process of mourning, there should be no set standard, no defined process that conveniently wraps up the story of any person's life. It should always be about remembrance. Life is not something lived in a clever thirty-minute sitcom package or movie-of the week presentation. Sometimes it pans out, sometimes it doesn't. We don't like it when somebody dies before the end credits roll but unfortunately, that's how life sometimes happens. Sometimes people just die. For many, television is the only exposure they have to that harsh certainty and it's not very representative at all so when reality happens to hit close to home, it hits especially hard. Nobody can turn the channel to make it go away.

Obituaries and funerals are limited by editors and practicality. Because of that, outsiders reading about any death in the paper rarely grasp the significance that one life had on the lives of those who knew the deceased. People anticipate clearly defined beginnings and neatly packaged, if not somewhat solemn endings as they read about the life and times of (insert any person's name here). Real life doesn't work like that. A person's life and the memories left in his or her wake are not items that can be conveniently summed up in two paragraphs or less or in thirty-second sound bites. Nobody's life happens in strict 'A-to-Z' order but we are accustomed to expecting precisely that. Everybody lives happily-ever-after and returns next week at eight. Nobody wants to accept reality. If a story doesn't end well, we don't want to read it; unless it's about somebody else.

How people deal with death is an extremely personal experience, affecting each and every one of us in enormously different ways. There are far too many variables to explain the reasons for how we all embark in the bereavement process the way we do, however, two factors glare acknowledgment; relationship and circumstance. The way people react to the news of a death depends essentially on those two things. How well did you know the deceased and in what manner did the deceased die?

I didn't know a soul buried out in that depressing little cemetery out there on the delta, but I stopped anyway. I paused, and I took a moment to wonder. I sat in my car on that old dirt lane and thought hard about the soldiers buried there, their families, and wondered how long it'd been since anybody thought about those souls interred beneath the little granite slabs in front of me. More people should stop during the course of their harried lives and do that; take time and pause; if not to remember, then at least to wonder. Because without anybody to remember, the memories of those who've died fade in vain; just like, as it seemed, all those people in that little cemetery I chanced by on the delta.

For all the brilliant revelations running through my mind that afternoon, I endeavored to create a project that didn't so much describe any actual battle scenes or plans or attempt to regurgitate anybody's brilliant tactics of destruction or reconstruction of my generation's war but simply to tell a story about an all too-often unseen and oft ignored after-effect. What happens when war is over? Who decides which side won and by what standard? What then? I wanted to fill in a blank that few to no books or movies have so far. What happens when all the little soldiers don't come home? What about what's left after extending heartfelt condolences to family members after someone they love dies? I snatched one moment from a survivor's life to show that although war related, Emily's Robert E. could be about anybody's experience as a survivor after a loved-one dies.

When an author details a great deal of information before a story's' actual beginning, editors call that back-story. A general rule of thumb is, "Don't write it until it's necessary and only put it where you need it." The whole reason why this book even exists is because of such back-story. In this case, it's called history. Besides, stories don't just pop into people's heads. Something has to happen, some precluding event that inspires a person to sit down and actually write about it. How many years did we end up fighting in Iraq this last time? If you never went there, then such back-story shouldn't seem so inconsequential.

So about all of those books; the events of September 11, 2001 and the subsequent war in Iraq gave rise to another predictable string of books, movies, documentaries and other miscellaneous made-for-television programs attempting to paint for all of us 'back home' pictures of the way life was for our soldiers stationed 'over there'. Such creations weren't all specifically about Iraq and Afghanistan, either. It seemed suddenly that any story about war was big business. Along with all of the tactical, opinionated, editorial and personal stories also came strings of war-related memoirs written by or about soldiers, written about the days/months 'in the lives of' bits as well as ambitious documentaries inspiring series about bands of brothers and sisters. Most abundant appeared to be biographical accounts; movies and television programs written by and regarding glaringly angry, pissed-off soldiers inclusive of some of the harshest red, white, and blue cursing that anyone could imagine, going well beyond the almost expected, "What the hell?" and, 'That's total bull-!" Not to minimize anybody's experience with the war in Iraq, (or any other country for that matter) but just how liberally does 'M-F this' and 'G-D that' have to be sprinkled through a book or script to drive a point home?

Many may feel some of those books, movies and memoirs about Iraq and Afghanistan tiptoed to a certain extent around the real reason the United States felt so compelled to dive into the Middle East in the first place. Many people thought the war in Iraq happened solely because of the events of September 11, 2001 while others believed the war had to do with oil. In the beginning, nobody had any idea how deep the water really was or how long the haul was going to be. People back home only knew what they were told in the days and weeks following the start of the war via seemingly nonstop news coverage appearing on every channel. As the war steadily turned from months to years, more books and commentaries appeared; ones decisively pro or con in sentiment regarding Iraq. The trouble with all of those though was that the conflict in Iraq was not one that could be simplified so easily into terms of black and white.

First came the tactical publications; books written in true military form by past commanders and generals comparing this war with the first Iraqi war of 1991, talking about current strategy and maneuvers, about how the United States was going to win, win, win the global fight against terrorism. Then came more personal tales; books written by soldiers or by the families of soldiers who shared their experiences on many levels about what they'd personally gained or lost; the soldiers after being called to duty, and the mothers and fathers describing how war had so changed their sons and daughters. Next, after a few staged military performances were exposed, came books defending and declaring the righteousness of the United States' occupation of Iraq, opportunistically grandstanding our country's duty in the war against terrorism.

For whatever reason, view, or sentiment, one point seemed to always be driven home; if we hadn't gone over there, the war could have come over here. People were going to die either way. That was the part nobody wanted to hear. Little could we foresee how there would be one more point as equally if not more important that would need to be acknowledged:

Did we learn/accomplish anything by what we have done?

Although on paper, the war was finally over and September 11 occurring what seems a life-time ago, it should be a given that we would never forget those who gave the ultimate sacrifice; but neither should we forget the survivors. The war will never be over for them. The point continuously (but not quickly enough) changed from, "How do you remember?" to "How should we remember?"

In the opening days of the Iraqi War were daily news stories and scores of all-purpose articles available informing readers of our country's supposed progress and then, NEWSFLASH! Somebody brilliantly proclaimed, "By the way, as a country, did you know (or even care) that we were never more vulnerable or less protected as a nation stateside than we were when thousands of our troops were deployed overseas?" (No kidding. How many billions of tax dollars did we spend figuring that one out?) Despite all the support and patriotism exhibited by Americans after 911, it didn't take long for people at home to become complacent, even cynical about Iraq. War was war. Lots of people went to fight in the name of defending America's freedoms, and some of those people died, all in the name of what? The World Trade Center? The Pentagon? Weapons of mass destruction? Terrorism? It was war, after all and no study needed to be conducted to predict that more people were going to die.

Everybody had an opinion about Iraq whether they were physically there or not. Some who actually fought there developed egotistical attitudes about having 'been there, did that' while many back home remained blissfully unaware;

that is, until something happened that affected them directly. Maybe it was seeing the family down the street tying yellow ribbons around the trees in front of their home or maybe it was another funeral procession accentuated by a group of Harley riding Patriot Riders heralding huge American flags for the neighbor boy, the one who just graduated with your daughter last summer. Maybe it was more personal, like losing a family member or friend on one of those ill-fated flights that hit the World Trade Center or the Pentagon? Or maybe it was just because...

Weapons of mass destruction? (WMD) Did we ever find any? The war on terrorism? Let's count the ways we justified fighting a war about a concept instead of a specific person or country; then add to that the years and years of over-saturation of carefully selected and censored media accounts on the nightly newscasts across the nation. Too soon, there was nothing fresh to read about or listen to, just daily American casualties to acknowledge. Thanks to censorship, political correctness, and the technological wonders of this century, the war in Iraq became one unlike any other America had experienced before. The explanation wasn't for any reason listed above as much as it was for the demographic making up the participants in this particular war. It wasn't only America's sons and husbands answering the call to fight in a foreign land. Unlike wars preceding it, this one saw more women doing battle right along with the men all in the name of defending the USA.

We became overly accustomed to living lives in an era of instantaneous communication. Something would happen at Point A and everyone at Point Z would know about it before nightfall. Gone were the days when messages took longer than 'right now' to reach their intended destination. Gone were the days of cold telegrams and reluctant taxi drivers delivering messages to unsuspecting recipients back home. We were in the time of cell phones, Internet access and death notification teams.

"We regret to inform you..."

Time; what a concept. Ideally, it takes an entire lifetime for a person to prepare for that unavoidable destination, the one we're all fated to. We choose to believe that we have "decades to prepare for that final ostentatious display of our lives; the long motorcade, the far-reaching admiration that few will ever attain." Sometimes, a lifetime simply isn't long enough, and tomorrow is never guaranteed to any of us. When somebody dies, time becomes irrelevant. In every circumstance, time becomes something either too long or not enough. It's something that simply marches on; unaffected, unaware.

All of those books and movies? Well, here's a story telling about more than what met the eye. In any war are numerous things that the common folk, the civilians never get to see or hear about until decades roll by, generals die and records get declassified. As far as the public goes, we get told what we're supposed to hear when we're supposed to hear it, given to know 'just enough' about circumstances in the meantime to keep us from getting too curious and told not to worry, Uncle Sam is going to take care of everything.

The back story here was quite necessary because after the war was declared over, Iraq was already the farthest thing from anybody's minds...unless you lost somebody there. War is about more than death and dying. It's about the other side of the survivor's mirror and the resulting experiences faced during an uncertain moment in time. Remember, quite often we are reminded that death is the only thing certain. Life is not.

18

CHAPTER 1

WHERE IT FIRST BEGAN

Long before there would be a history of Emily and Robert E., there first was this one…

A long, long time ago, a quiet, unassuming farm boy living in the foothills of Arkansas's celebrated Ouachita Mountains met a pretty little gal from the nearby town of Mena. The quiet, unassuming farm boy was a fine, upstanding citizen and along with many other young men his age, enlisted in the military, departing for "the halls of Montezuma" and "shores of Tripoli" prepared to go to battle in a country he'd only heard about on the radio.

Theirs became the classic boy meets girl, girl falls in love and boy goes to war story. While the quiet farm boy Marine was fighting for his country, the pretty little gal back home wrote faithfully to him every day he was away. When the quiet, unassuming farm boy returned, he and the pretty little gal from Mena who had written to him faithfully every day, got married and started a new life with one another. He was 22 and she was just 19.

Over the course of their modest lives in the mountains of Arkansas, the pretty little gal gave the quiet, unassuming farm boy five beautiful children (well, make that six…six beautiful children). "Let's name our little surprise Wilhelmina after the lodge on the mountain. We'll call her Emily for short."

They were not of the wealthiest means but the burgeoning family was a prosperous one. The quite farm boy Marine and his pretty little gal from Mena gave their brood everything they could, everything they had and the children gave back in return. They each worked diligently, earning good grades and becoming fine, upstanding citizens in their own rights in the very town their mamma and daddy had. Everybody knew the Nichols kids and the Nichols kids knew everybody. That was the way their lives unfolded as far as life in the small town went. There were enough of them too, those Nichols kids, all six of them accomplishing the goals they'd set for themselves in school and sports and unselfishly taking part in different activities within the community. It was little surprise that every single one of them attended college on scholarship, each earning their respective degree before moving away from the mountains. The Nichols kids did well and began living lives of their own in the world beyond those famed foothills of Arkansas. All but one, the little surprise child. Wilhelmina. She had bigger dreams…

This was where the story of Emily and Robert E. truly began.

CHAPTER 2

EVERYBODY HAS A STORY TO TELL

"The incessant rush of time deprives our lives of so much dignity and meaning. It is, perhaps, more than anything else, the arrest of time that gives certain pieces of work their feeling of depth and significance."
Williams

Their Fates were so deeply intertwined that neither of them could have ever imagined to what extent, how profoundly their lives were in synch. With their story, there was no concern for political correctness or general suitability. It simply was what it was; nothing less, nothing more. Other than the obvious "Never forget", there were no earth-shattering lessons to be learned or revelations to be made, no poignant morals to convey. (Never mind the fact that people quit caring anything about morals years ago.) There were no heroes or villains here either, at least not in the typical sense; no action-packed, explosive or even remotely loud drama either. Emily's Robert E. was purely a necessary account in need of being told.

Theirs was a tale about one Marine, two hearts and a thousand aching 'what if' moments revisited. It wasn't a simple matter by any means, especially not with all the questions that invariably followed these two in their wake. Out of all those questions, one was always easy enough to ask but almost impossible to answer: why?

Constant distractions. Obscure emotions. Obscenities; three things that were constantly on Robert Elliott's mind. Why the obscenities? Deep in thought, Bob Elliott once again found his mind wandering to places that seemed vaguely familiar but with no idea how he'd gotten to any of them or why. It wasn't a physical unfamiliarity so much as it was a mental haze, an unwelcomed sense of déjà vu. He found himself reaching for, trying to focus on such hit and miss thoughts numerous times over the years. Ever since he'd left 'Middle-of-Nowhere' Arkansas for the first time over twenty years ago, he'd lost count of the number of times such unscripted dreams and ardent thoughts had exploded into his mind with no rhyme or reason, vanishing just as suddenly. Today was one of those days.

"Knowing my luck, it's probably low blood-sugar. Lucky for me it's nothing a burger and an ice-cold beer can't fix." Bob brushed off the repeated moments of vagueness, continuing whatever task happened to be at hand.

At the same time, nearly seven thousand miles away, Emily Nichols was sitting in front of a laptop thinking about the quirky web site she'd inadvertently scrolled across a few nights previous as she'd taken a routine stroll through cyberspace. Humming softly to herself she'd grinned as she paused to read through the site.

"Ingenious. I wish music would play during epic moments of my life too, just like in the movies. Imagine the soundtrack to that movie." Emily easily recalled several appropriately larger-than-life moments from her life with songs to match.

As she navigated through the website, Emily was almost embarrassed by some of the information people had posted. "Why do folks advertise such personal stuff for the whole world to read?"

In Iraq, going for a typical insomniac run wasn't a ready option. Besides the sweltering heat (or freezing cold depending on the moment/time of year), Emily rationalized that wandering through cyberspace was probably a much safer alternative anyway; at least at that insane hour of the morning.

"What I wouldn't give for an ice-cold beer or a burger from Dairy Queen right now."

Neither of them had any idea that somewhere in the world, somebody else was thinking the exact same thing. Even before graduating and leaving their outwardly unremarkable hometown in Western Arkansas, Bob Elliott and Emily Nichols shared more in common than accidental thoughts. Theirs was something more than Fate; something more than simply, 'meant to be'. Nothing less. Nothing more. Or was it?

"Isn't this just the story of my life?" Bobby lamented out loud more than once. "Always a day late and a dollar short."

Half a world away, Emily took in a deep breath letting it out in a slow, impatient sigh.

"Sure. Everybody has a story to tell. Isn't that the truth." Emily closed her eyes in deep thought. "Just happens there's no one around to hear mine at the moment."

CHAPTER 3

EMILY'S ROBERT E.

All the seemingly chance events occurring in Emily and Bob Elliott's lives weren't as hit and miss as they believed. Each chapter of their lives connected them to the next without so much as a table of contents or the convenience footnotes to guide them. Some folks might have called it self-fulfilling prophecy but according to Fate, things happened in life simply because they were 'meant to be' and Emily was a big believer in Fate. For her, there was no such thing as coincidence. There were no clearly defined beginnings or endings to any part of life; at least not to the naked eye and for her and Bobby, 'meant to be' was certainly the case. For Emily, circumstance had to be just right before the eventual meaning of life with Bob Elliott became clear. She couldn't find the right word to explain what she felt. Obsession wasn't right. Fascination? Curiosity. Whatever it was, it was something present in her life ever since Mena.

Emily and Robert Elliott's tale was one unfolding against outwardly impossible odds with life's lessons coming to light only after 'happily ever after' was long out of the question. Too soon there would be only empty reminders sprinkled with those much talked-about, highly-doubted hints of déjà vu. Theirs was about how almost cosmic connections spread profoundly across the bands of infinity and though definitely tested, could never truly be broken. Besides, how could two such unsuspecting people ever have known the number of times or under what circum-stances their paths would continuously cross? For Emily and Bob, it became a matter more about the journey than the eventual destination. If only by virtue of what was going on in the world around them at the time, their story was something more than 'meant to be'. It was one that had to be. As simple as that sounded, it turned out to be quite the contrary. For them nothing was ever that easy...or simple.

The morning of September 11, 2001 had already dawned in America. It was a day destined to begin like any other. Kids had been dropped off at school, mothers and fathers dutifully went to work while still others had set off to go grocery shopping, jogging in their favorite park or do whatever else it was they had planned to do that morning in cities and towns all across America. Trouble was that as far as that evening went, some of them wouldn't be coming home. Designed to begin like any ordinary day, the morning of September 11, 2001 turned out to be anything but.

With 911, the world had unexpectedly become a much smaller place. That morning shortly before nine o'clock Eastern Standard Time, America found herself questioning how the Fates could have been so aligned. The assault was at first incomprehensible and disbelief swelled across the nation in suffocating waves. By that night in the momentous hours following the astonishing violence, three things became markedly clear. The continental United States had been attacked for the first time since the war of 1812, America was up in arms and the powers that be began discussing preparations for war.

"The United States will stay in Iraq for as long as necessary but not one day more."

Marc Grossman

CHAPTER 4

IN THE REAL WORLD

The public loves reading stories about 'the other guy', no question about it. In fact, it doesn't matter what the information's about; the good, the bad, or the ugly. But let's face it; it's mostly the ugly which people care about most. There's always been and will always be individuals being 'glad it wasn't me' or 'wish it were me types' when it comes to 'blah, blah, blah.' (Insert favorite event/ worst nightmare back there.) Especially true, more than any of it unfortunately, is the tasteless but very typical convention concerning people enjoying the hard luck of others.

But what about that bad and ugly? It's a disheartening fact speaking volumes about any society as a whole, though in America, one well-substantiated as evidenced by the number of rag magazines stuffed into check-out racks at every large-scale retail chain on the planet. In truth, nobody likes to read about winners or inspirational success stories of the little guy. People pretend. Not as many people care to read the warm and fuzzy human-interest stories as they do the tragedies. All people really care about is the low-down and dirty, period; not the cute and cuddly. Folks enjoy seeing others put up against themselves because it makes them feel better about their own insecure lives. As far as the public is concerned, it seems that the more dubious and detailed a story, the better. Bizarre is just a plus. "Aliens Land in Hot Springs" or "Bigfoot Sited at Oklahoma Border" trumps "Drunk Driver Arrested at Hayden Springs" any day. Nobody wants to read the stuff about ordinary Joe Schmoe unless it's the unfortunate minutiae regarding how he lost his house and where his daughter really went when she left town last summer. People don't seem to ever get enough about the current events or issues that really should matter either, at least not enough so as to miss the valid points at hand... or do they?

There's generally an assuring comfort, an almost indisputable sense of belonging and attachment to a community when a person can open their local paper and read about the people he or she knows. Just as easily, anybody easing through said small town can quickly learn about the outwardly unremarkable lives of the locals simply by picking up the paper and skimming through police briefs or studying the society pages and let's not forget the infinitely popular engagement and wedding announcements section, too.

All that interesting society stuff aside, there's a part of those hometown newspapers that reveals much more about members of its community. It's the section we all end up in sooner or later, later being the preferred objective. It's usually the last, though certainly not the least most interesting part of the paper; the obituaries. Let's face it, despite the fact that it involves a modest bit of journalistic voyeurism, reading through those little biographical sketches tends to induce and inspire some mildly poignant if not downright visceral emotion. (Never mind the occasional, unscrupulous lot of scammers and con-artists.) There's no censorship, no prejudice, no preordained order to names appearing there, at least not if you don't count the occasionally alphabetical order some editors prefer to arrange them. No matter how hard one looks, sometimes there's just no obvious rhyme or reason to those notices.

Nobody's life is a solitary chapter, a simple story that can be conveniently wrapped up between "once upon a time" and "the end." Such stories are called fairy-tales for a reason. One life is never about just one person, but no sense in getting overly analytical about the obituary page, right? "Calling hours will be this evening from five until seven. In lieu of floral tributes, please make donations to the local humane society." When you're dead, you're dead. That's it, the end of somebody's story that in an ideal world took seventy-five to a hundred years to create, gets summed up in two paragraphs or less then that's it; all over. People gather, services are held, the departed is buried and everybody goes on living. Actually, that's not it; not entirely.

There's no such thing as anyone dying a natural death anymore. Doctors continue playing God and relatives continue refusing to accept why Great-Uncle Silas didn't get up for coffee this morning. There always has to be an underlying reason why so-and-so died. What's the scoop on that Henry Jones fellow; the one the paper said died after a brief illness? Brief illness? Who do they think they're kidding? Nobody dies that young without a reason. Probably had cancer; nothing brief about that. Hear 'bout that kid over in Tahlequah? Prime of his life. Heard he took his car for a header off the I-40 Bridge; probably drunk. That's all the kids around here have to do, you know. And did you hear about Widow Lemmon? Still sharp-as-a-tack, even at a hundred and one. She finally passed away. They said one of her grandsons found her sitting on the front porch swing with ice still floating in her tea.

"That's the way I want to go."

"Glad it wasn't my kid" or conversely, "That could've been my kid."

"Hope I'm still livin' on my own like she was."

No matter how anybody dies or how it's written up in the paper, there's always the predictable extra two cents that gets thrown in by somebody whether they knew the dearly departed or not. How many people continue wondering or in the very least speculate about the other people mentioned in those orderly, alphabetically arranged biographical sketches on the back page? The survivors, the next of kin? Maybe a week or two rolls by before the dearly departed is forgotten, disregarded by everybody on the outside who may have chanced to be looking in on the occasion in the first place. The lucky ones will be remembered in some local parades still being held on Memorial Day before everybody goes out to get drunk at the family picnic. And as for the rest?

To the so-called 'Entitled Generation', Memorial Day means nothing more than a government-sanctioned excuse for a day of inebriation. To those who served in the military, Memorial Day still serves as a reminder. Remember that number? Roughly only ten percent of Americans can claim the status of Veteran. People stop thinking about such things because they want to. After all, who wants to give consideration to the thought of dying?

Survivors may expect, even times anticipate the death of a loved one but what about the people nobody expected to die? What about the people that don't get the chance to live 75 to 100 plus years? What about the people looking out from the inside that, no matter what amount of time passes, are left wondering, waiting, and expecting? What about the people left behind?

Not long after the events of September 11, 2001, all across America, in the small towns and villages particularly, an unfamiliar type of obituary began appearing with a frequency not last seen for thirty years or more. If one took any small-press paper across the nation and looked on its' obituary page, chances are that within the past few years somebody in 'Such-and-Such' town or backwater 'Burg knew somebody who 'died over there'; in Iraq.

The names of World War I and II vets that once graced those pages had already become forgotten. There weren't many old boys left who'd fought against the Germans or the Japanese. We fought a war against Germany? When'd we do that? Where is Normandy anyway? Allied Forces? What's the deal about December 7? Pearl Harbor?

Names of Viet Nam vets eventually took a turn, becoming commonplace for a spell. Ho Chi Minh? Cambodia? What was the significance of that wall of names in Washington? And what about Bosnia, Somalia? Where are those countries anyway? Why were we fighting over there in the first place?

War had become a comfortably foreign concept, if not an entirely forgotten one to Gen X'ers, the so-called 'entitled' generation of America. For the most part, the idea of war where people get killed, where somebody isn't coming home was forgotten, except by those who had fought in or lost somebody to one. And then, of the soldiers who had went to fight and were fortunate enough to make it back, some of them continued fighting personal battles long after their particular war ended. War has never ended for some.

Hosts of military campaigns have been choreographed throughout the years with lives senselessly lost to 'Name

Your Favorite Conflict Here' between the last World War and the first war in Iraq. Operation Urgent Fury, Just Cause and of course, operations Desert Storm and Restore Hope as well as Operation Enduring Freedom. Who remembers those campaigns besides those who fought in them or the families who lost loved ones to them?

We were not long into the first decade before 911 became a painfully familiar term, an overused phrase of the day, an understood reference regarding the terrorist attacks on the United States that began on September 11 at the World Trade Center in New York. Thus had been laid the groundwork for what came to be known as Operation Iraqi Freedom; the war in Iraq. The events of 911 meant the subsequent 'global fight against terrorism.'

Prior to the events of September 11, many Americans had already planned on enlisting in the military because they needed money for college or they wanted to get out of Home Town, USA for whatever other reason that came to mind. Some people didn't expect to have to actually fight a war in some country they'd barely ever heard of, much less cared about. Then it happened; September 11. It didn't matter if a person was in his last semester at college or somebody's wife was expecting their first child next week. It didn't matter some of those people who'd enlisted a month ago with the uncomplicated intention of getting an education just outright didn't want to go someplace where it was 'kill or be killed.' It wasn't long before troops were put on alert, reserve units activated and America was headed to war.

"Make no mistake…" How many times were those words dropped on the American public? Once again, we became a nation involved in a war, a conflict on another foreign shore.

As far as opinions about that war, we became a nation in disagreement amongst ourselves. Then seemingly overnight, names of pre-twenty and thirty-something's started appearing in obituaries across the country. For the most part, names of privates, specialists, and corporals (depending upon which branch of the military they had enlisted in) were displayed with painful regularity and only occasionally were the names sprinkled with the likes of a Lieutenant or Sergeant-First-Class. Familiar names started gracing those final pages too, their military service noted with little flags by their names, dying in service to their country. People didn't know whether to feel proud, guilty, or glad; proud that their son or daughter had served, guilty their sons or daughters didn't die or secretly glad that somebody else's did. It didn't take reading any kind of paper to figure out how people felt.

CHAPTER 5

NOT SUCH A SMALL WORLD AFTER ALL

We've all done it to some degree. Whether it's been from the comfort of our living room sofa or from a cafe hundreds of miles across the country, people have tried keeping up with whatever was going on back in Hometown with all the Wilson's, Jones's, and Johnson's that they knew. Preferably, we liked doing our eavesdropping and peeking from afar, from some comfortably distant place; invisibly, unannounced, undetectable and were secretly (or not so secretly) glad when the bad things happen to somebody else. Sometimes though, in undecided, unexpected reflection from somewhere deep within the wrinkled recesses of our despicable minds, somebody occasionally stopped to ponder; "Should I have felt guiltier about a particular fact? Should I have taken the time to feel blessed that bad stuff didn't happen to me? I'll worry about that tomorrow; if at all."

About those small-town newspapers…that was how Emily Nichols kept up with her Hometown, USA; by reading through the on-line version of her local paper. On any given day of the week, she usually found herself scanning through headlines in the papers' on-line society section just to see who was getting married or buried. It was a little disheartening to say the least when Emily discovered the newspaper had been sold again. It seemed like it'd just been bought out not all that long ago.

"How long before "Hometown News" gets printed someplace like Bangor, Maine?" Emily muttered to herself. She chuckled as she imagined a telemarketer sitting in a cubicle in Bangladesh speaking broken English.

"Hello. Mr. King? How are you this evening? Sure some crazy weather we have there this week, no? Would you care to take a subscription to our Morning Time News?"

Sitting idle and waiting for life to 'just happen by' had never been part of Emily Nichols' philosophy. After all, half the fun of doing anything in life was the seeking. Life was too short to just sit and watch. Frequently, Emily took the time to deeply reflect on her past, looking back at the years of her life with a rare longing. More often than not, she'd marvel at how far she had come, reminding herself that hers was not the typical 'small town girl' existence. She lived by one simple rule; minimize your regrets.

As much as she had wanted to get away from the little town she grew up in, Emily often found herself reading the Hometown News to keep caught up on the goings on back there. One disheartening aspect was that the people she read about were growing less and less familiar as the years went by. At one time, she could have given directions to just about anybody's house from any point in town but too many people had died or moved away since she'd last been home. Emily was sure the day would come when she wouldn't recognize any names in the paper.

Her parents courtship had evolved around a place in the Ouachita Mountains named for Holland's Queen Wilhelmina of all people and almost inescapably, as the surprise child and youngest of six, Emily was named accordingly. Though Wilhelmina Nichols went by the less attention-demanding name of Emily in her everyday life, she was no less strong-willed as her namesake was purported to have been with an energetic yet quiet character. Emily was a real go-getter, a self-proclaimed 'mover and shaker' who spoke and acted her mind accordingly.

Experience had proven to be a wise teacher and Emily soon outgrew the life she'd found herself resigned to living in Mena. She began making her way through life outside her parent's small, country town, thinking she couldn't wait to leave on a permanent basis and never stayed in one place for very long. But such as the case usually goes, she always went back. The newspapers' on-line columns weren't the only way Emily kept up with news from back home.

Like every other person in the world, Emily'd had her share of interesting, if not to some extent, insane experiences fall her way. She'd never felt she had points to prove to anybody and was always ready for the next challenge that happened her way. Emily was the type of person who'd go first and ask questions later. Granted, some people might not have considered some of the things Emily'd partaken in her life to be of the brightest caliber but all that colorful history was what made Emily's life so distinctly hers. The biggest event she ever aspired to which she had absolutely no regret about was her decision to attend the United States Naval academy with aspirations of becoming an officer in the Marine Corps. When Emily received her commission, nobody had been more surprised than herself. The East coast wasn't prepared for the whirlwind that blew in from the Midwest.

Of the many journeys in her life, one of the more peculiar things Emily had quickly became aware and amazed by was the general lack of knowledge people had about the world around them, apparent in some who wore it almost like a badge of honor instead of recognizing the condescending air of privilege that so few bothered keeping to themselves. Every community had some; individuals who rarely, if ever ventured from the fifty-mile radius of where they lived, ate, and breathed (and would eventually die) yet professed to know all the ways of the world, condemning anybody else for not being just like them. It was a peril of coming from a small town and also the very reason Emily wanted to get out and experience the world in the first place. The comfort of people and places familiar was nice but Emily needed more. The military fulfilled that feeling.

It was an early autumn afternoon back in Arkansas, one that found Emily enjoying unseasonably warm temperatures. The weather couldn't decide if it wanted to completely allow the effects of fall to firmly take hold or if it would tolerate a few final days of summer. As pleasant as the temperatures were, cloudy with the slight chance of rain had made for Emily brewing a comforting cup of tea and taking an unexpected stroll down Memory Lane.

Some people kept scrapbooks and photo albums; others simply journaled about their lives, but not Emily. Over the years, she'd collected a variety of keepsakes, exclusive memorabilia embracing assorted photos and scribed journals, keeping them in a red, cedar box, a gift from an old friend made long ago. As she lived her life, Emily filled that box with an assorted compilation of mementos and souvenirs, collecting the seemingly trivial but certainly essential bits and pieces of her life as it curiously unfolded around her. In that box were things that anybody else sifting through would have no idea of the meanings connected or associated with her life. The cedar box became proof of the diverse life she'd breathed.

How the red keepsake box itself came into existence was a story Emily warmly remembered each time she carefully eased back it's' lid. An old friend, a master carpenter who was a real genius when it came to woodworking, had agreed to create the custom-made project. She literally had begged and pleaded with him for a number of years before George finally got around to drawing up the plans. When he at last presented her with the gift, she was speechless. It had taken him so long to make that Emily had all but given up on ever getting the finished product. It promptly became one of her most valued possessions.

"If I'd known how quick it would shut you up, I'd have made you one years ago." George joked. Secretly, he'd been quite proud of his work. The red, cedar box ended up meaning something special to him too, as she was only one of a handful of people left in his life who could boast knowing him, "from decades ago." He felt almost honored that Emily had cared enough to want something crafted from his design.

Emily breathed in the familiar scents released as she opened the box, allowing herself to be transported in time. Resting on top of the collection of memories was a recent picture. Though it wasn't taken very long ago, the photograph was one a hundred years in the making. She tenderly removed the photograph of the railroad trestle, its image reflecting on shimmering water below, glancing casually at the writing on the back. First, in script that most would have considered uncharacteristically ornate for a man, was written the date and name of the place they had stopped and then her own writing, where she had unhurriedly scribed, "Our very own bridge of

Madison County." Emily closed her eyes deep in thought, remembering that weekend vividly.

It was July, hottest month of the year and the place was a mutually agreed upon location in Central Oklahoma, an area they were both very familiar with. The town's location was best described as one between the latitudes of Fort Smith, Arkansas and Wilburton, Oklahoma; places farther east they'd visited that same weekend. The Oklahoma location had less to do with lines of latitude and longitude than for the fact it was the place the dart had landed when Emily threw it. (And yes, she'd eventually told Robert E. she'd really thrown one.)

At the same time that day but in a different place, Robert Elliott's mind had casually wandered from his task. He too, had taken unexpected pause that morning reminiscing about the reunion he and Emily Nichols shared earlier that summer. Over the years, Bob found his thoughts increasingly focused on his former classmate and despite every effort, couldn't figure out why. After all, Emily hadn't even attended their high school reunion, the event he, himself had originally returned home for. He started thinking about the visit the two of them ultimately shared in July after the class reunion had come to pass. He'd scolded himself countless times since because he'd never mustered the courage to tell her everything that was on his mind. Bob Elliott had never been the shy type but around Emily Nichols, he felt a vulnerability like he'd never felt with anyone else. She was the main reason he'd decided to attend the high school reunion in the first place. Rob felt more than a little disappointed when she didn't show. He knew she was back in town and wondered why she hadn't attended. He'd found her number easily enough, thinking long and hard before making the call, unsure if it was even a working number. He wanted to ask her if she might meet with him before either of them left town again.

He thought he knew exactly what he was going to say, too what he wanted to share with her but each time he started to dial the number, he'd lose his nerve. Bob finally let the call ring through, almost dropping the phone when he heard her voice.

"Okay, but only if I get to pick the place." She'd agreed at the last minute. "I'll throw a dart at a map and see where it lands. If you agree to the location, we can meet for a cup of coffee or something."

By the time their visit had drawn to a close, Bob Elliott still hadn't summoned the courage to tell Emily the way he felt, had always felt about her. He thought that visit was going to be the one. As it turned out, it took a little more time.

CHAPTER 6

BEFORE THE COUNTDOWN BEGAN

Before arranging to meet in Oklahoma, Emily had been sitting cross-legged in an overstuffed chair in her living room in Mena, deep in reflection. It'd been yet another afternoon that found her relaxing with a trusty cup of hot tea, absorbed in recounting various memories from the past, something she did with relative frequency. She was feeling wistful again, reflecting the changes of the little town of Mena and thinking about the days and people in her life gone by. It was the place Emily'd learned to gradually understand all of the life lessons her parents had exacted upon her and her siblings as they were growing up, lessons their parents had learned over the course of their own lives and passed on to all six of their children.

She hadn't recognized the number when the call rang through and almost didn't answer the phone. The last thing she wanted to do was allow herself to be pulled away from the pleasantries of daydreaming by some telemarketer trying to sell magazines.

"Hello?" She answered cautiously.

"Emily? Emily Nichols from Potter Junction?" The voice at the other end of the line sounded hopeful.

As Emily recognized the voice on the other end of the line, her breath caught and she felt her heart skip a beat.

"Maybe. May I ask who is calling, please?" She knew full well who it was.

"This is Rob-, I mean Bobby Elliott."

"What a pleasant surprise." Outwardly, she'd responded cheerfully. To herself, Emily immediately wondered why he was calling and how he'd gotten her number. It wasn't as if they had talked a whole lot after high school. They'd been friends, even dated some but Bobby Elliott always seemed too busy being a jock to ever acknowledge the crush she had on him.

"Thought I'd try droppin' you a line. Actually, you caught me by surprise. I didn't expect anyone to answer. I was just going to leave a message. Anyway, I, well, I'm going to be in the area for a few days, not quite in town but, well about as close as I planned on getting' again 'til spring. I've got something over in Santa Fe. The thing is, well, I heard you'd made it home. I wondered, since you missed the class reunion if maybe you'd like to meet up for a cup of coffee or dinner or something, play catch up? I know it's been awhile and you probably don't have the time what with me calling so out of the blue like this but-"

"Sure." Emily interrupted.

"Emily?" The voice asked again.

Distracted, Emily wasn't aware that she hadn't answered his question out loud, wasn't even sure she'd heard correctly the question the voice on the other end of the line had asked in the first place. After all the years that had passed, how could it possibly be him? How at that precise moment when she was already reminiscing? She was trying to process the call, no easy task considering that the thoughts in her head were racing a hundred miles an hour.

"Well okay. Sorry to have interrupted your day. I guess you're-" Robert E. tried not to sound disappointed.

"What?" Emily interrupted again. "I mean no Bob. No, I mean yes. Sure. We can get together. That sounds great," Emily was flustered, caught off guard by the unexpected call. "But only on one condition..."

Already in a melancholy mood, it wasn't hard for Emily to draw up memories of Bob Elliott. It seemed too many years ago to count but just before the beginning of their final year, a group of seniors had decided to get together for a bonfire at somebody's cottage at the lake. From out of the blue, Bobby Elliott had asked Emily to be his date. Without a second thought, she had accepted. That weekend turned into one full of many surprises. Everybody had a great time, so great in fact that Emily thought something more might finally develop between she and Bobby Elliott. They went on later dates throughout the year all the way to graduation. Despite the fact they'd dated, it seemed clear to Emily that Bob Elliott would always have one foot stuck in that high school persona. His attention quickly turned to SAT scores and baseball, concentrating on where the best college he could get into was. As far as anything permanent ever developing between them, nothing ever did; not then. There was rank and file structure those days and Emily'd determined never to be part of that scene. But somehow she knew that she and Bob Elliott were destined to run into each other more than once. She didn't know when and she didn't know how but Emily knew.

CHAPTER 7

ALWAYS HELLO BEFORE GOODBYE

Bob Elliott had already made plans to be back in town but for an entirely different reason. He'd been through Arkansas earlier that spring but prior to that, it'd been years since 'Robert E.' Elliott had actually gone 'back home'. It wasn't until around class reunion time that he'd heard on grapevine authority that Emily Nichols was going to be in town as well. Two people who decades ago wouldn't have known the other still existed (he was a contractor managing a job in the extreme northwest and last he knew, she was a Marine stationed somewhere in Iraq) reacquainted via that modern marvel the Internet. Considering it was the Internet, their ability to reconnect wasn't such a remarkable feat, really. The fact they'd attended high school together in that fabled land of 'Long Ago and Far Away' made Emily consider his surprise phone call something more along the lines of Fate, plain old meant to be. Bobby Elliott didn't believe so much in Fate. When he'd dialed the number he'd found on the internet, he hadn't expected to reach her so easily.

Their initial meeting went well, entailing well more than a simple cup of coffee.

"I liked your picture." Emily's voice was just as soft as he'd remembered. "You don't look the same. Familiar enough though. I mean, well what I mean to say is of course I knew it was you but-" She'd trailed off as she realized she was babbling. He hadn't stopped her, simply sat back and listened. Of course she'd known it was him. She'd been keeping up with Rob Elliott as much as he had with her. It wasn't hard to do coming from the little town they'd both called home, though she never expected to find herself planning any sort of reunion with anybody from their graduating class, much less Bobby Elliott exclusively. Emily had always assumed she wasn't his type. After all, they'd had all senior year to figure that out.

"Post office? Milk cartons? Internet? What's the difference? A picture's a picture." The ice was officially broken as he laughingly lit a cigarette. "Just so you know, there've been so many Rob's, Bob's, Bobby's on job sites that when I turned supervisor, I started going strictly by Robert E. Keeps things a whole lot simpler up on the scaffolding." He had sensed a not so subtle hint of nervousness to Emily's otherwise self-assured manner.

"Robert E. Oh. I get it. Like the general?" She smiled. "Started smoking too, I see."

"Ah, about that. We all gotta die of something, right? I blew out my knee not too long after getting that scholarship. How's that strike you for Fate? Anyway, playing ball was out of the question. Didn't have to worry about being able to run bases anymore." Robert E. paused wistfully. "I figured what the heck? Already had all the paperwork done so I stayed there, finished school, got my degree and started working construction shortly after. That's when I started smoking, too. I didn't need a Bachelor's to do what I ended up doing but it felt good knowing I had one in case something else happened and I couldn't work a job site." Silently, he wondered how to tell her how he'd been keeping up with her over the years without sounding like a stalker. It wasn't as if there were hundreds of Wilhelmina Nichols to sift through in those wild-card searches on the Internet. Finding her was easy enough but even with the hometown advantage, he'd still lost track of her shortly after her parents had died. Emily'd essentially dropped off the radar which for her was nothing surprising. She'd always been that way, always present, never saying or doing anything to draw attention to herself. Emily'd always hung back, never getting involved with anything or anyone. Regrettably, Robert E. had only recognized her presence after she was gone.

"So what's with your profile? How come you didn't post any old pictures?" She waved a stray wisp of Robert E's smoke from in front of her face as he chuckled. "None even for old times' sake?" She studied him discreetly as he chain-smoked his way through half a pack of cigarettes. The sleeves of his Wrangler brush popper shirt were rolled over strong, tanned forearms that reminded her of old Popeye cartoons. It appeared that the construction trade had been exceptionally good to Robert E.

"Been lots of years, Em. I figured anybody who knew me back then wouldn't have any trouble recognizing me now. Those pictures may be goodies but remember, they're oldies too. It'd been a little deceitful, don't you think?" He grinned as he offered her the cigarette in his hand, knowing full well she didn't smoke. "At least I still have all my own hair. Can't say the same for some of the guys in our class," He took another nervous drag from his cigarette "-or some of the gals, for that matter. I have to admit though; I do like shaving mine off every once in awhile, whenever the mood strikes me." He grinned, not realizing he was still offering the cigarette to her. "How about you?"

"Nope. Never had the mood strike me." Emily smiled. "I like my hair long."

Robert E. grinned a boyish smile. "No, I meant have you run across anybody's profiles?"

"Hasn't been on my top ten list of things to do and really, no thanks." Emily shook her head emphatically at the cigarette. "Guess Fate wasn't going to be denied." She smiled and stared across the parking lot before them. "What in the world made you decide to look me up after all these years? How'd you even know I was stateside?" She looked into his eyes. "Must've been Fate at work again." Emily remembered enough about Robert Elliott to know he didn't put stock into any particular religion, much less Fate.

"Fate," He snorted predictably. "Believe me, it wasn't Fate. It was a whole lot simpler than that. It was class reunion time and you weren't there. Nobody'd heard from you. I'd heard rumors you were in town. Small town, don't forget. It's not like we had a big class, anyway. I mean, lots of people asked if I knew where you were, wondered if you'd really turned into a Marine. I've tried keeping up with what all you've been doing, at least over the last few years, you know." He wasn't sure if she'd caught that last remark. "You know, you're the only gal from our class who went into the Marines. Probably the only one who could handle their boot camp, though that's just my opinion, of course. A few people even thought you might've gotten killed in Afghanistan." He knew he was starting to babble but continued talking in a nervous banter. "Hey, remember Jeff Havers and Andy Finch? They're both doin' pretty well for themselves. Jeff's got his own trucking business and Andy's still around Mena somewhere working auto body or something like that." Robert E. was quickly running out of things to say. He paused, taking a slow, deep breath before continuing. "You know, there's been one or two guys from a class behind ours who've been sent home," Robert E. stopped himself. "-well, you know. They had big parades for them over in Ft. Smith." Quickly changing the subject, he continued. "Who'd have thought little Wilhelmina Nichols would wind up in the military, period? And as a Jar-head of all things?" He referenced the military photo she'd posted on the social website. He'd known full well Emily had received her commission thanks to all the news clippings good old Mrs. Rainey continuously sent him.

"I've never been one to believe in Fate." He nervously bounced between subjects. "I mean, life pretty much goes the way we lead it, don't you think? What was it you always used to say?" They sat in silence, each wondering what the other was thinking.

"We are masters of our own Fate, to a certain degree. But it doesn't matter what I think. I know I believe in Fate," She emphasized 'I'.

"So you weren't satisfied with just going enlisted, huh?" He grinned, trying to change the subject. "Sorry. You know, you ought to be careful talking about them Fates in the middle of the Bible belt, Sweetheart. Believin' in Fate is sacrilegious." He joked with an exaggerated southern accent, not realizing she was still serious. "So just how many years has it been now?" Robert E. let the question trail. Emily remained impassive but listening in attentive silence, the 'you could have heard a pin drop' kind. He had no way of knowing how much her thoughts had lingered on him through the years.

During the course of their conversation, they discovered their lives had paralleled each other's in extraordinary ways. Despite the many years and miles between them, Robert E. couldn't help but feel that they had still somehow managed to share common bonds. Chewing thoughtfully on her bottom lip, Emily continued studying Robert E.'s features as he spoke. Other than a few lines around the edges of his ever-sparkling blue eyes, Bobby Elliott, or Robert E. as he now preferred to be called was still as handsome as she remembered.

Figuring she didn't have anything to lose besides another decade or two, Emily took a deep breath. Despite the fact that it was he who'd called her, she'd to tell Robert E. about the feelings she'd had for him since their junior year. Never being one to dive right to the heart of a matter, she first asked him a question.

"Robert E.? Have you ever wanted more than what Fate was prepared to give? You know, like not wanting to wait to see what kind of dirt they had up their sleeves?"

"That's right, there were three of 'em, weren't there?" Robert E. blurted as surprisingly enough, he remembered taking some obscure class in mythology. "Fate isn't just one person." He took a long, thoughtful drag from his cigarette. As he thought he was discreetly evading her question, she was thinking that he was missing the point entirely. Silence sometimes spoke volumes. Though she'd been secretly pleased by his out of the blue phone call, she didn't know what exactly she had expected from the subsequent visit.

"Yes, the Moerae were actually three sisters who acted like one entity better known as Fate. Wow. You actually know that?" She was genuinely surprised he possessed such knowledge. Back in the day, Rob Elliott seemed to have been more interested in sports and cars then he was with absorbing any off the wall information.

"Actually, yes. Yes I do." Robert E. sat back looking pleased. He even surprised himself sometimes. It wasn't as if he'd been especially fond of the class. "Why are you so surprised? The Moerae were actually necessary evils. I mean, they weren't evil but you know, in order to be a well-rounded student, I couldn't just take the core curriculum and run. You might remember those classes called electives?" Robert E. laughed. "I'm sure you had your share of 'em." A sudden 'a-ha' look crossed his face and he nodded his head. "The Moerae are the gals who decide human fate. I get it now." Emily's viewpoint of the world. "Okay. Let me see if I can remember them right. There was Cloris-"

"Clotho." She corrected.

"Cloris, Clotho, whatever. Lachesis and Atropus. Lachesis was the one in charge of things that were, Clotho handled the things that are, and Atropus was in charge of things that will be. Every person has their own set. Mainly, Fate's all about one moment at the end of everybody's life and the circumstances leading up to it. But Em, I have to tell you. Death's the last thing I want to talk about." Robert E. nervously lit another cigarette. "Anyway, to answer your question, I don't want more. I mean, I don't want Fate or God or whoever to think I'm a greedy guy." He sat there silently lamenting his lost opportunities from years ago. No sense worrying about things you can't change, Robert old boy. She'd never consider the dating game now. No sense in even going there. He waited patiently for her to respond.

"Well I do." Emily answered with quiet but powerful determination. He looked at her, surprised by the tone her voice had taken. "Robert E. I've planned, intentionally chosen most everything in my life, choosing the way I've wanted it to roll ever since I was old enough to care. I've always known what I wanted and worked my tail off to get it. I've done things my way despite the fact there were people always a little eager to tell me how everything in life couldn't be planned or counted on. Silly me, I never accepted that. I always wanted more. I'm still not prepared to let Fate or Cloris Leachman have the final say." She smiled at her reference to Robert E.'s faux pas. "Call me the greedy one then. I don't care if God or anybody else thinks I'm being so. I know that's not the way everybody thinks life is supposed to go but I've never been like everybody else. I've always tried living life with minimal regrets, never wanted to be one of those people looking back wishing they'd have done something they only let pass them by."

"Well at least you're not bitter." He raised his brow and grinned. "But I see your point. I've always liked that about you. You were never a follower."

Pin-drop silence again; a little uncomfortable this time. What was she trying to say?

"Minimize your regrets." If she only knew about all of his regrets. That was the precise moment something clicked between the two of them, something good. "Some pretty sound advice there, Em but what about Fate?" He grinned. "How do the Fates fit in with all you believe?" She didn't have an answer for that.

CHAPTER 8

THE PERFECT STRANGER

As he had told Emily, he went strictly by Robert E.; not Bob, Rob, or Robbie anymore and most definitely never 'Bobby' (unless it was his folks.) Just Robert E.

"Thank you very much."

He was named after the Confederate general of the Civil War but had never made the connection until he was out of school. His mother had been a Civil War buff back in her younger days and had determined to name all of her children after famous figures in history. Robert E.'s mother was a proper little southern woman born in the early 1940's just south enough of the border town of Texarkana to be able to claim she was a Texan by birth. What mattered was that despite the fact that the original Robert E. was a gentleman, he was also, without a doubt a force to be reckoned with. True to her interest in the Civil War, Robert E.'s mother decided the same would be said of her youngest son; Emily's Robert E.

Actually, as amazing of a presence he commanded, the original Robert E. Lee wasn't very fearsome in his appearance. The man wasn't even six feet tall. On the other hand, Emily's Robert E. was an imposing 6'3, Mr.-Clean looking fellow, right down to his occasionally clean-shaven head and gold hoop ear ring in his left ear. Years ago, if you'd chanced to catch him on a bad day, he'd have hoops in both ears just daring somebody to comment. He was handsome and clever, a very charismatic sort of fellow usually with a temperate nature. But let him knock back a few long necks and Robert E. turned downright contrary. (Emily only saw that side of him once.). More often than not, Robert E. was by and large a heck of a guy to have around. Emily had always been infatuated with that boy back in school and had thought, often daydreamed about the man Robert E. had surely become.

To a certain extent, Robert E. was indeed relatively comparable to his Civil War namesake Robert Edward Lee. He didn't have any ties with the original fellow of course, but Emily knew enough about the famous Civil War general to draw more than a few comparisons between the two. She knew there was a memorial to Lee in Louisiana located in New Orleans standing on a pillar of marble purposefully facing north. The reason for that exact position was because it was General Lee's belief that a man should never turn his back on his enemy. Lee's enemies, of course were the Yankees. Emily's Robert E. never turned his back to his enemies either which was what usually got him into trouble. He was heard a time or two to say it was your enemies you needed to hold on to most tight "-'Cause you never knew who's liable to slip up behind you carryin' a Louisville slugger or somethin' worse. I've had a few knots beat upside my head 'cause I didn't pay close enough attention. You never know when somebody's gonna try taking a swipe at ya."

Though it happened what seemed a lifetime ago, the Oklahoma reunion set into motion a chapter which could have more easily began with the time-tattered, overly used 'once upon a time' or 'in a land far, far away.' Instead, it was by chance that Robert E. had located Emily again in the first place. Together they fell back into step on a journey designed by circumstances beyond their control, continuing a story that had its beginnings long before they'd ever met.

CHAPTER 9

STILL DAYDREAMING

Emily continued sipping slowly at her cup of tea. Theirs wasn't a conventional story by any means. She remembered after that surprise phone call how she and Robert E. had planned their impromptu reunion and how quickly things had transpired thereafter.

"Must've been meant to be. How else can you explain it?" She mused.

It'd been years since graduation, years since they were both living in the same state, but because of a tip from Hometown and a successful search on the Internet, Robert E. had been able to locate Emily quite easily. On little more than a whim, after she failed to show at the class reunion, he'd decided trying to call her and see if she'd care to meet with him for a cup of coffee, leaving the decisions of if, when, and where entirely up to her. For whatever reason, old feelings had motivated him and Robert E. became determined to find Emily Nichols again. He wasn't even sure if she was still in the service. Emily hadn't been overly concerned about revealing any details of her life, military or otherwise when they'd first spoke on the phone. After all, it'd been a long time since they'd seen one another.

To her, there wasn't any need for exchanging complete life histories, at least not to that depth of detail. Emily had literally thrown a dart to decide where she'd meet her long-lost friend and when she suggested the location, he'd agreed. The dart landed precisely where Emily had aimed. The destination of their ensuing reunion had its origins around a man-made lake in Oklahoma called Eufaula; a location little over one hundred miles from where they'd schooled together, a location familiar to them both. She wondered if he would remember.

"What a perfect night. Look at all the starts." Emily spoke so quietly that Bob Elliott almost didn't hear her.

"If you keep watching long enough, I bet you'll probably catch a few of them falling." Bob Elliott hadn't been sure if Emily Nichols would be interested in a bonfire at the lake and was surprised she'd agreed to go with him. He didn't think she was usually one for crowds. In fact, he couldn't remember her ever going out and doing things with anybody from class. Emily was one of those girls who was likable enough but kept to herself. Most people thought she was a little snobbish but Bob found that couldn't have been farther from the truth.

"You want to build our own fire over here?" Emily asked softly as she blushed in the night, realizing how that must have sounded only after she said it.

Bob Elliott apparently hadn't taken notice or heard her as he grabbed her hand and pulled her toward the bonfire.

"Come on. Let's help throw some more wood on the fire."

Emily shrugged her shoulders and smile.

"Sure. Let's go."

CHAPTER 10

IT WAS OKLAHOMA

Robert E. wasn't surprised when Emily asked him to meet her in Eufaula. He could think of a dozen other places he'd rather they'd have met but kept those thoughts to himself. He hadn't realized how the little town of Eufaula had grown since high school and as surprised as he was with her choice of location, it turned into a most fitting place to begin their spur-of-the-moment visit after all.

"She could've said no." Robert E. mused as he waited for Emily's arrival. He was thrilled that she'd agreed to meet with him to begin with. Truth of the matter was, the dart she threw could've landed in Rhode Island or off the coast of Oregon, it wouldn't have mattered. Robert E. would have driven whatever distance was necessary to meet up with her.

As he waited in the parking lot, Robert E. began to alternately grip and release the steering wheel in anxious anticipation. He'd been so nervous during the course of their last conversation that he'd failed to ask what kind of vehicle she would be driving.

"Relax, Robert." He chided himself. He wasn't overly concerned; positive he'd recognize her on sight. "It's Emily

Nichols we're talking about. Emily Nichols. Emily. Em-" He trailed off.

It wasn't long after the first wave of regulars left when a silver Lexus pulled into the lot, parking next to the building's entrance. Instinctively, he knew it was her.

Whistling through his teeth, he slowly shook his head. "Well what do you know? A Lexus?" Robert E. asked himself in disbelief. "Why not? Would've bet odds on a pick-up, though." A smile played at the corners of his mouth as he passively watched Emily exit her vehicle. Emily unhurriedly locked her door then progressively swept the parking lot with her eyes. She paused at the sporty rental car; his rental car.

Robert E. called out his open window. "Howdy stranger."

Emily's face lit up instantly. "You're not growin' any taller just sittin' in your car." She greeted in her unexaggerated Ozark accent. You could take the girl out of Arkansas but you couldn't take the Arkansas out of the girl.

Robert E. slowly got out of his car. It'd only taken them little over a decade but here they were, in Oklahoma of all places. With barely contained excitement, Robert E. forced himself to close the space between them in slow, deliberate steps. First squeezing her in a warm embrace, he stepped back and took an appreciative look at her.

"You look great." They exclaimed in unison.

"Ready for that cup of coffee?"

Together, they walked arm in arm into the cafe adjacent to the Holiday Inn, the only cafe open in town as far as Robert E. could tell. Other businesses on the block were still closed but at seven-thirty, the little cafe was hopping as its' second wave of regulars started to arrive.

"Looks like we got here just in time." Robert E. spoke out. "I'd almost hate to see what this place is like when they're really busy." They quickly claimed a corner booth and ordered coffee, falling effortlessly into conversation.

"Do you remember the last time we were here?" Emily asked as she emptied her cup.

"Ah, so there was a reason the dart landed in Oklahoma." Robert E. remarked as he without doubt remembered. "Here. You mean Eufaula, right? As in I know there wasn't a Holiday Inn here back then." He motioned to the waitress for more coffee. "You need a shot?" Emily nodded her head, acknowledging his question but her mind was already a million miles away, or at least back in another chapter of her life. It was that night at the bonfire years ago. Unknown to either of them, that particular night was Fate setting the groundwork for future memories of Lake Eufaula and Oklahoma. Who could have guessed she would ever find herself in Bobby Elliott's company again, especially with all the years that had passed between them?

"You know, you still owe me." Emily was sure Robert E. didn't remember.

"Owe you? For what?" Robert E. sat back and studied her. He wasn't sure if she was being serious or not. "I owe you what? A favor? Money?"

"No, no favors and definitely not any money. If you owed me money, do you think I would have let you wait how many years to pay me back?" She studied his puzzled expression.

"Then what do I owe you?" Robert E. poured sugar into his coffee as he searched his memories. A puzzled expression furrowed his brow. He thought he'd figured out why the dart had conveniently landed in Eufaula, but now he wasn't so sure.

"Tell me you don't remember?" Emily leaned forward conspiratorially, motioning for Robert E. to do the same. "Think Robert E. Think back a long, long time ago. Think about the lake." Still no flicker of recognition crossed his face. "A campfire, the lake. You owe me one. We never took our campfire by the lake."

Furrowing his brow again, Robert E. sat back. "The lake."

"The reason this town is called Eufaula?" She chided.

"Oh, that lake." Of course Robert E. knew the significance of the location she chose. It just took him a little extra time to remember. It would have been too simple to meet in Mena. "If I remember correctly, it wasn't Lake Eufaula though. We were up at Tony Scott's cabin for a bon-fire." The memory slowly came back to him, but Emily had already changed the subject.

"So, what have you been doing with yourself over the years?" Emily started flipping through the menu on the table. "Want to order some breakfast?"

Conversation inevitably turned from the reunion Emily had missed to events leading up to her becoming an officer in the Marines.

"So why didn't you go?" Robert E. asked her, referring to the recent class reunion.

She shrugged her shoulders and responded simply. "Didn't get an invite." Her response came out more sarcastically then she had meant. It was clear to Robert E. the recent reunion was not a subject she especially cared to delve into. Not entirely comfortable telling him about her life in the military either, Emily tactfully changed subject. "I'd like to freshen up before we start trying to figure out what we're going to do." Emily waited for his response.

"Sounds like a plan. One problem though." He finished his cup of coffee.

"What's that?" Emily flipped a couple of dollars out on the table for a tip.

"I don't think check-in is before three o'clock."

"Not as big of a problem as you may think." She looked at her watch and grinned as he made a face. "Let's see what we can do about that. Maybe they'll let us check-in early." He looked at her dubiously. "All they can do is say no, right? Besides, it's only three, four hours. I'm sure we can find something to do in the meantime. Didn't anybody ever tell you to question everything?"

Despite the fact that check-in was indeed three pm, Emily managed talking the clerk into letting them check-in early.

"You just filled yourself two more rooms than you thought you were going to five minutes ago." She cheerfully thanked the clerk. "Two less empty rooms. We won't tell anybody you let us check-in early. Thank you."

They elected adjoining rooms with a spacious balcony overlooking the lake. "Robert E., how about we eat breakfast out here in the morning and watch the sun come up? When's the last time you actually watched the sun rise just for sake of watching a sunrise?"

He shook his head at her and shrugged his shoulders. "I watch the sun rise every day on my way to work." He grinned as she looked at him with questioning eyes. "You forget. I'm a construction worker, up with the birds, before the birds sometimes. I do more before ten o'clock then most people do all day."

"That's the Army's old slogan." She teased.

"Come on. Let's go down and get our things."

Robert E. helped Emily remove her bags from the trunk of her car. "Since we're this close, I thought maybe we could hit Branson. You know, take it easy getting' there and catch whatever sites we happen to see along the way."

Later that afternoon…

"Mind if we stopped here a minute? I've got to get a picture of that." Little did she know how the simple, nondescript photograph Robert E. was about to take would capture a moment in time neither of them would ever lose.

Not one to ever take the well-beaten path, Robert E. had decided to take a few left turns along the way instead of going right. In the process, they'd found themselves on a scenic byway in the extreme northwestern portion of Arkansas. Robert E. had caught the old rusted, railroad trestle out the corner of his eye about an hour after they'd left the Interstate that morning and had made a mental note to return to Eufaula the same way. For some unexplained reason, he felt compelled to come back to the bridge.

Emily had taken notice of multiple signs along Cripple Branch Road that warned, "Caution: Winding and steep." As it turned out, the signage was an understatement. Besides winding and steep, the road was extremely narrow as well, leading Emily and Robert E. down a more southerly route as they made their way back to the Interstate.

Robert E. slowed the rental-car to a stop, automatically reaching into the back seat for his camera. As he prepared to open the door, a tractor-trailer with Oklahoma plates that they'd been playing leap-frog with all morning barreled down the hill, passing them with a thunderous roar, shaking the aged concrete span the car was sitting on.

"Good riddance. I was getting' sick of that guy doggin' our tail. What's a semi doin' on a road like this anyway?" Robert E. shouted to Emily's side of the car. "That's the same guy who was trying to get ahead of us ever since we left Harrison."

"How do you figure that?" Emily asked doubtfully. "We stopped about an hour for lunch. It couldn't be the same guy."

"Girl, you need to look further than the hood of your car when you drive." Robert E. commented. "It was him, I tell ya and I'll tell you something else, too. I bet we pass that joker again up on the Interstate before nightfall."

"I guess it's a good thing I'm just a passenger then." Emily stuck her tongue out at Robert E. "Tell me again why we stopped here?"

"That." He pointed out her side of the car. "Look. See that old railroad trestle? I saw it this morning when we came through but I didn't notice the reflection on the water. The whole scene struck me, you know? I just felt like I needed this specific shot." Actually, Robert E. couldn't explain why exactly he had felt so compelled to get that particular picture. It was another one of those thoughts that randomly popped into his head, something he felt compelled to do.

"You know, in Alaska, when you take any road less traveled, you're apt to find places you'd swear were fresh out of the 1800's. I mean, working up there, I've had a lot of opportunity to go exploring. Depending on where you go and how much time you can take, you might find some old mining camp, or abandoned logging site, especially down around where I'm working right now. All sorts of things get left in some pretty far-out places. I'm talking about troughs, dredges, cranes; I mean, I've seen mining equipment that looks straight out of the original gold-rush days. But then again, I suppose some people call the entire state of Alaska off the beaten path, period." Robert E. paused, taking a breath before continuing excitedly. "My point is that there's all kinds of roads to follow, to get lost on. Alaska's full of great places to explore but you've got to be real careful how you go about doing it. Now, this here with the reflection on the water like that? Beautiful."

She grinned. "All that just to explain why you wanted to take this picture?" Emily knew Robert E. was nervous. "How many times have I heard you say 'Hold on a sec, I'm pulling over? I've got to get a picture of that' today?" She'd lost track of the number of rolls of film he'd used since they started out that morning. "You need to invest in a good digital camera. I mean, who even develops film anymore?"

"A guy I know in Denali wanted to move some major inventory and gave me a great deal. Told me if I bought all the film he had left on the shelf, he'd develop it for me at cost. I can always scan the best pictures later." Obviously distracted, he commented, "A person can observe a lot just by watching, you know."

"I imagine that's how most people do it, too; observe by watching." Emily smiled at Robert E.'s unintentional play on words. "You can observe a whole lot, especially if you know what to listen for." Robert E. was concentrating too intently on the bridge to notice Emily's teasing remark. She sighed in exasperation. Changing the subject, she asked another question.

"Did you by chance happen to notice the name of the county we're in, Mr. Elliott?"

"That's Mr. Photographer to you, Ma'm." Lowering the camera, he chuckled, "Wait. I didn't say that right, did I?" Robert E. looked at her with a sparkle in his eye. "And sure I noticed. It's Madison County."

Emily studied his expression.

Robert E. busied himself with taking the picture. "Take a good look around. This is some of rural America at its' best. I'd almost forgotten what this state looks like. We haven't seen a single McDonald's or Wal-Mart in the last twenty miles and you know, this is even the state Wal-Mart originated in. Alaska's got the mountains, I mean big, beautiful mountains but they're more along the lines of blue and gray; lots of blue. That's not sayin' we don't have -" he trailed off as he absorbed the picturesque view before them. "I'm babbling again."

Though dusk was well on its way, Emily was still able to admire the many brilliant shades of green enveloping them from every angle.

"Do you think Ireland is like this? You know, they talk about forty shades of green?" She commented as they continued making their way down the mountainous road. The flourishing canopy sported a single power line to spoil its' continuity. As the sun prepared for its descent, Emily began to catch the distinctive chorus's and refrains of peepers, the little tree frogs especially numerous in the lower lying areas, as they chirped their evening song.

"Ignoring me again?" Robert E. asked as he slid back into the drivers' side. Emily had been intently concentrating on the scene before her, inhaling the lingering scent of his cologne. She thoughtfully breathed in his words before responding.

"Sorry. You were saying?" Emily quickly blushed, embarrassed he'd caught her daydreaming, more embarrassed that it was about him.

Robert E. remembered the long pauses Emily took to respond to questions as he suddenly understood the hesitance he thought he'd heard in her voice when he'd first called. She had probably been thinking of the best words to answer his with. People who didn't know her often took the trait as a sign of pretentiousness. That assumption couldn't have been farther from the truth. He'd learned quickly she wasn't one to squander words and when she spoke, what she said was generally something of worth. Some things hadn't changed.

"Ah, it was nothing. Let's get going. It's going to be dark soon and I want to spend some time just kicking back and relaxing before heading out to Santa Fe in the morning."

"You're still going?" Emily asked with surprise.

"Well, it's one of the few places I've never been. I'm this close so I figure why not, right?" Robert E. wasn't sure but thought he detected a trace of disappointment in her voice.

Knowing their visit would soon be drawing to a close, Emily and Robert E. sat up talking throughout the entire evening. Time ceased to exist as neither noticed the mercury-vapor lights blinking on one by one around the hotel. Filling each other in on their lives after graduation, they stood at the balcony railings looking at the stars, each harboring thoughts about the past and debating, wondering how to bring those things into the present. Neither one of them took notice as those same mercury lights started blinking out across the lot nor the new day dawning on the horizon.

The morning broke with the sun lazily making its appearance over the lake before them. From their vantage point on the balcony, Emily and Robert E. watched as brilliant streams of sunlight danced off the waters' surface, scattering like spilled diamonds on waves that rippled gently to the shore. They knew their reunion was about to end but neither wanted to be the first to acknowledge it.

"Check-out isn't before too long, you know." Emily commented offhandedly as she nonchalantly glanced at the Timex on her wrist. She watched as a little Indian woman started loading her housekeepers' cart with cleaning supplies, freshly laundered sheets, towels and complimentary packs of decaffeinated coffee.

"I know." Robert E. responded after his last swallow of juice. "I know." He sat back and looked at Emily. "Morning sort of sneaked up on us, eh?" He'd been watching her with fascination, curiosity, and unashamed anticipation. Her skin was still flawless. The delicate smell of her perfume mingled in perfect harmony with the soft scent of honeysuckle wafting from the tangles of vines entwined in the lakeside hedge below. The morning was pleasantly cool but he knew the sun would soon ride high in the sky with no shade to be found anywhere.

"So." He was watching her lips move but hadn't heard any of the words she spoke. His thoughts were on that campfire he'd promised her so long ago but never delivered. The significance of Lake Eufaula hadn't escaped him.

Emily sensed Robert E. was deep in thought and turned her eyes back to the vast expanse of water before them. She saw ducks bobbing on the lake without a care, a train beginning to meander unhurriedly across tracks in the distance, and fishermen already easing their shiny, fully-loaded bass boats into a few shady coves readying to concentrate on the task of just 'being'. It was the perfect start to another lazy day in July. Several minutes passed before Emily broke the silence that had settled so comfortably between them.

"Bobby? You doin' all right? I mean, how've things really been for you?" Emily continued her impassive observation across the lake and watched the train slowly disappear from sight. He probably wasn't going to take the question seriously. She was still wondering why, after all the years that had passed, had he decided to contact her? Their lives had turned too different, too complicated. In her own mind, Emily questioned to herself yet again; am I reading too much into this or what? People don't just decide to look you up ten years after graduation without a reason.

"You mean like, satisfied with life in general? With the journey to where I am today? What?" Robert E. knew it was a loaded question and was careful not to answer her too quickly, too flip. He placed his hands behind his head and closed his eyes. Though Emily had always been philosophical, it had taken him over a decade to figure it out. "I guess I'm pretty happy with where I'm sitting right now, figuratively as well as literally." Better say something clever right now, Bobby old boy, he thought to himself. "What makes you ask?" Ever since they'd met at the cafe, he'd sensed she had a lot more on her mind but didn't want to pressure her by mentioning it. He knew she'd speak her mind in due course.

"It's hard to explain." Emily paused. "I mean, we all have our little happy place we try to get to. You know, the place you go to think about things, or where you go to get purposefully lost in memories, remembering the old days or thinking, wondering about how you've gotten this far in life? I mean honestly, like today. I've been wondering why, after all these years, over ten years Bobby why you decided to just now get in touch? I mean, not that I haven't enjoyed our visit but..." Emily's voice trailed off. She didn't know what she expected. Ten years was a long time.

Robert E. waited patiently. When a full minute had passed and Emily still hadn't added anything, he opened his eyes and turned his head in her direction. "Hey, where'd you go?"

"Happiness; put it in a bottle and slap a label on it, right? That way, you know where to find it the next time you need it without having to work so hard to get it." She looked into his blue eyes, waiting for him to tell her he was feeling the same, looking for some sort of sign. "Stick a patent on that and you'd make a million in no time."

"We make our own happiness Em. You know lemons and lemon-aid? Life hands out lots of lemons, sure but so what?" He paused, trying to decide how to answer her question. "It's like what you said, about how you've tried to minimize regrets. We all have choices, right or wrong, we make our choice one way or the other. We make the best choice that we think fits the situation at the time. I mean," Robert E. paused again, "- I guess what I'm trying to say is that we all have a direct hand in choosing which way our life is gonna roll. Do we turn left or do we turn right? Once we decide what road to head down, we still have another choice; how's the rest of my life gonna go? What's my life gonna be? It isn't going to be lemonade all the time," He paused mid sentence. "-wow. Where'd all that come from?" He laughed it off. It's now or never, he thought as he turned his chair to face Emily directly.

"So how far is it to Santa Fe?" Emily asked, changing the subject. He'd never answered the original question.

Without missing a beat, Robert E. sat back easily and responded. "Six, maybe seven hundred miles." He'd lost his train of thought, forgetting that he wasn't really going to Santa Fe after all. He couldn't tell her that though. She'd think he'd planned it.

"Seems like a long way to go if you plan on making it before dark."

"Em?" Robert E. pushed his chair back and leaned toward her. "When we leave here, can I call you again?"

"Sure." Emily smiled, confident that he would not. "You've already got my number." Their difficult lives and the thousands of miles weren't the only things between them this time. He had no idea that she'd only been home on leave, or that she was currently debating whether or not to make the moment before her a reality.

"Em? What would you say… well, what I mean, what I'd like to ask you is-" Robert E. knew it was a make-or-break moment. A lot of things could go wrong, but at the same time, something could go so right.

Emily knew by the way he was stumbling with his words and his loss of eye contact that Robert E. hadn't anticipated this particular moment. Neither had she. It simply happened.

"Why don't we ask for late check-out?" She said softly, making more a statement than asking a question.

That weekend ended much too quickly as far as Emily was concerned. Though many years had passed, they still shared plenty of common ground. Despite how well their reunion had unfolded, Emily determined that Robert E. was just as complex. She wasn't sure if they had accomplished anything more than what two other mutually consenting adults would have under the same circumstances. Regardless, it would not be something she regretted.

"Maybe it's all been in my head. People don't simply start looking for someone, find them then start talking about 'can I call you again' for no reason." Emily had grown more confused than anything. There were several moments during the course of that weekend that she thought Robert E. was about to reveal something important to her but that 'something' never came into being. Other than their impulsive moment together, Emily wasn't sure what to think about Oklahoma.

Later that afternoon as they readied to leave their respective ways home, she still hadn't determined what thoughts had really been playing on Robert E.'s mind and he never offered revealing them. Little did she realize there were several moments as they loaded their vehicles that he was thinking the same of her. Robert E. watched Emily, thinking she looked ready to say something but she never did. As quickly as they had planned it, their visit was over.

"You probably want to gas up at the truck stop before you hit the Interstate." Emily offered as she closed to trunk to her car.

"You too." Robert E. didn't know what else to say.

They left on the same Interstate, opposite directions never talking of commitment or future plans.

"Story of my life, I suppose." Robert E. expressed to the empty space around him. He watched his rear view mirror as the silver Lexus slipped further from his view. He couldn't know it but she was doing the same thing, watching him slip from sight in her own mirror. As he watched her car ride almost out of sight, Robert E. picked up his cell phone and dialed her number.

He hesitated. "I wanted to ask you something."

Emily waited patiently for him to continue.

"Yes?" She finally prompted.

"Will you call me when you get back over to Mena? I'll want to know you made it all right." That wasn't at all what he had planned to say.

"Only if you'll do me the same favor. Call me when you get to Santa Fe. Don't be a hero and try driving all the way. Pull off somewhere if you have to and catch a nap. Nobody will bother a sleeping Sasquatch." Feeling let down, Emily forced a laugh to hide her disappointment.

Robert E. made west for Santa Fe as Emily headed east toward Fort Smith and highway 71; same Interstate, opposite directions.

"I'm going to regret not telling him for the rest of my life." Emily briefly debated calling him back.

"She probably wouldn't have taken me seriously anyway." Robert E. lamented as he watched Emily's car at last disappear from his rear-view mirror.

Unknown to either of them, Oklahoma was to be another beginning, a new chapter of their lives and the continuation of another, longer journey they'd both been destined by Fate to embark upon. Despite more time and greater distance, the road would eventually lead them back to each other one more time. They had managed bridging all the lost years during that unexpected weekend in Oklahoma, as if time hadn't left either of them behind, had carried them together despite the separate paths and years between them. They'd finally reconnected, were finally on the same sheet of music and almost on the same note. Neither of them could know how world events would shape their lives.

Robert E. couldn't explain it, but even the occasional silences that had fallen between them during that weekend were charged with an almost emotional depth and hidden meaning. To him, it was as if they'd been reading each other's mind all along.

As Emily made her way back to Mena, she found herself distracted as she drove by the familiar sights they'd passed together only hours before.

"This is ridiculous." Emily spoke out loud to herself. "I mean really, what did I expect?"

Once again, it was a not-so-simple matter of Fate; two Fates actually. How else could the timing have been so precisely right? The adventure in Oklahoma ended too soon and Robert E. eventually returned to the wilds of the Alaskan Frontier. He did call her and even dropped a few letters. But to Emily, despite his good intentions, Robert E. still seemed sidetracked. During subsequent conversations, it seemed as if he was distracted or rathered be doing something else.

She knew a long-distance romance could never work. He thought she was home for good and had no idea that was not the case. Emily never told him otherwise, having not been sure where their reunion was going to lead to begin with.

CHAPTER 11

EVER SUCH A THING

Emily continuously replayed the memories of that Oklahoma weekend in her mind. She thought about it often, scenes flashing in her mind without warning. That seemed to happen a lot, actually, one minute she would be thoroughly absorbed in some task or other than all of the sudden Robert E. would cross her mind. It was something she could never explain.

"Cup of coffee my foot." She smiled. Emily harbored no regrets about the way the weekend had turned at the last minute. "I wonder if this is what they meant when they say we make our own Fate?" Emily looked out the window. The weather hadn't improved and she was still dissecting recollections of that weekend, a weekend that already seemed so far away. The phone rang, startling her into nearly dropping the now empty cup. She stared at the caller ID. "Ask me again why I believe in Fate like I do?" Not for the first time that year, she smiled as she took a deep breath and answered the phone.

"I was just thinking about Oklahoma." Emily teased.

"Would you call me crazy if I said I know?" He asked innocently. Of course, it was Robert E. It seemed he had developed a sixth sense, some impossible way of knowing when she was thinking about him.

Their conversation started with standard pleasantries, exchanging small talk, (she hadn't gotten any better at it and he was never any good at it at all) like the seemingly requisite how've you been, what've you been up to and everything else they could think of in between before coming to a thoughtful pause, one she took as an invitation to enlighten him about how she felt.

If there was one thing deployment had taught Emily over the years, it was to never take tomorrow for granted. Too many times she'd witnessed the phenomenon of 'now you see me, now you don't.' She didn't want to make the same mistake in her own life. Tomorrow wasn't guaranteed to anyone.

"Robert E. Have you stopped to wonder about 'what if' yet?" She blurted. Emily had, lots of times. Things like what if her mother had been more brilliantly inspired to name her something like Lisa or Susan? But Wilhelmina? Nobody really named a child that, did they? Who named a child Wilhelmina in this day and age? It could've been worse. Thoughts of names like Elizabeth and Susan- names common in her mother's generation quickly came to mind. With regard to the uniqueness of her own name, Emily knew all too well the story behind it and had grown to appreciate the exceptionality it lent to her. It wasn't long before her thoughts drifted back to 'what if?' What if she and Robert E. had dated more seriously all those years ago? What if they had never moved away from Hometown? Had he intended on more than catching up when they met that past July? Though it was his every intention, Robert E. could never muster enough courage to tell her. Emily didn't know that. How could she have known that was exactly what he had planned?

Some things in his life could've been considered 'given' while other things he had to fight for by tooth and nail. Emily Nichols; could she have been either? Only Fate knew for sure and Robert E. already made it abundantly clear he wasn't one for believing in Fate.

"Wondered what if? What if what?" He asked absently. He was thinking about wasted years, all of the times he could have, should have made his feelings known to her. He thought about their visit that summer and wondered if she would consider any sort of relationship now? What if? He'd called her that particular afternoon on impulse, not at all prepared to tell her what he thought he knew he wanted to say. He really hadn't expected her to be home and had only a short message prepared to leave on her voice mail. When Emily actually answered, it caught him completely off guard.

She had been holding the photograph of the bridge in her hand the entire time they talked. She'd never told Robert E. she'd been looking at it, either. It was enough for her to relive the memories of that weekend and tuck them away, along with the picture, back into the red, cedar box that was her life. Emily knew better than to expect Robert E. to say anything that would make her stay. He hadn't yet but maybe this time…

"I'm babbling again and it sounds like you're multi-tasking. I've got a few things I need to finish up so-" She cut him off politely, finally making up her mind on the basis of that one call.

"I'll check back with you again soon, Em." Robert E. knew she had no idea why he had called and tried not to be upset by her offhanded manner. He was flustered and couldn't find the words to start over again in revealing his true intention.

"Sure. Maybe we'll get together again to play catch up, just so long as you don't make me wait another decade." She couldn't think of anything else to say. "Same place?"

Robert E. knew he hadn't accomplished anything by the phone call and as he hung up, he wondered if he should have just left well enough alone. In another state, miles away, he couldn't know that Emily was thinking very nearly the same thing.

The assortment of souvenirs and mementos Emily stored in the keepsake box changed very little over the years. The collection started out as just a few old pictures and newspaper articles she'd clipped from the local paper when it was still a Hometown press. It wasn't long before she'd added a little white jewelers' box full of dried poinsettia leaves. For sentimental reasons, Emily had collected fallen leaves from a plant she'd given her grandfather for the holiday's years ago. What started out as a joke and a tiny plant turned into a fond memory of her grandparents' old house on the hill. Her grandfather tended that sorry little holiday sprig until it turned into a hearty plant of titanic proportions which he proudly displayed in his living room year-round.

As the years passed, she added various other objects, things that held no meaning to anybody else. There was a favorite dogs' old collar and an antique Zippo lighter with gold inlay that once belonged to her mother, an heirloom of sorts not to mention assorted collections of old letters kept from key people in her life who'd long since parted; all in chronological order, bundled together according to who wrote them. As she gently tucked the bridge picture in with the rest of the photographs in the box, she gave a deep sigh. The cedar box was becoming more and more of a reminder of a part of her life that was gone forever. She wondered if that would turn out to be the case with Robert E.

It would be almost two years before the Fates chose to bring them together again. Between the moment they reunited in Oklahoma and their next encounter, they were busy living their lives in separate hemispheres, losing track of each other much the same as they had after graduation years before. Emily had quickly dismissed the unexpected weekend in Oklahoma as a flash in the pan, proving that perhaps some things weren't as "meant to be" as she'd once believed.

"At least I managed to minimize one more regret." She smiled to herself.

Unbeknownst to Robert E., Emily still had unfinished business to tend to regarding her enlistment with the Marines. She knew she wasn't getting any younger and she knew she wanted more out of her civilian life but making it into the Marine's was a goal she had worked hard to realize. She didn't want to totally give it up. Not yet. Whenever she was on leave, Emily always returned to Arkansas, to the town she once thought she couldn't wait to get out of. Though she had not planned it, it seemed the little town of Mena was destined to be the place that she would call home. Despite knowing where she was, Robert E. lost touch with Emily when she was deployed overseas to a desert thousands of miles away. Neither of them knew how long it would be before they crossed one another's paths again or under what circumstances.

CHAPTER 12

THERE AND BACK AGAIN

He watched from his vantage point atop the adjacent knoll as seemingly in slow motion the red, four-wheeled drive pickup first slid unexpectedly across the empty southbound lane and rolled easily over the embankment. There wasn't anything he could do but watch it go. The driver hadn't been traveling all that fast either, just dumb luck the truck had hit a patch of black ice. It didn't take much.

"First real snow of the year and it'd figure, wouldn't it?" Robert E. automatically let off the gas, slowing to a gradual stop as he approached the broken rail. He dutifully jumped from the heated comfort of his truck's cab, hastily pulling the hood of his well worn Carhart jacket up over his clean-shaved head. It was mornings like this he was glad he'd at least kept a full beard. Looking both ways, Robert E. quickly ran across the road and took his first good look over the side of the road. Peering warily down the side of the steep embankment, he was relieved to see the truck had at least landed on its' tires. "Not the first time I've seen a roll bar actually come in handy." Robert E. quickly weighed his options. He deliberated for only a split second before flipping his half-finished cigarette into the slush-filled ditch in front of him.

"What's the worst case scenario here?" He muttered to himself. "Find a couple of teenagers flung through the windshield or maybe save some guy on his way home from picking up donuts and the morning paper?" It was a bona fide wreck, had just happened and he had no idea who or how many people he'd find inside or what shape they'd be in. He knew what he had to do, beyond the fact that it was the right thing to do. He attempted to cautiously jump from the snow-covered pavement to the other side of the slush-filled ditch. Naturally, he fell short and his boots immediately filled with ice-cold water that rose over the sides.

"Son-of-a-" Robert E. cursed under his breath between clenched teeth. "Good Samaritan Act nothin'! Damn this all to hell and back! There should be a law-" He stopped mid-sentence, immediately feeling guilty about the string of profanity he'd just let loose. Though he was a grown man and it was sometimes in his nature, he knew if his Mama had heard him, she'd have had a word or two to say about his choice of words.

Disregarding the water now sloshing in his boots, Robert E. rapidly made his way down to the battered truck. Even from atop of the bank, he instantly recognized the red and gold foiled emblem strategically placed on the tinted rear window. Robert E. shook his head. "Semper Fi. Great." That was all he needed to deal with, some punk home on leave driving Daddy's brand new truck like it was still the middle of June, thinking he was invincible, refusing help and spouting off how he was a Marine and Marines were tough, and he didn't need any ambulance.

Without further contemplation, Robert E. reached the truck and cautiously peered through the broken driver's side window. Reaching into his coat for his cell phone, he realized he'd left it in his truck. Looking up the bank toward the guard rail, Robert E. debated whether or not to first run back for the phone he'd left tucked in the console or first see how badly the driver leaning against the door was injured. He saw remains of what used to be an airbag, obviously deployed.

"Ah, I know that had to hurt." Robert E. winced as he unconsciously rubbed the side of his nose, remembering wrecking a few vehicles over the years. Airbags saved lives, sure but didn't do too much for a person's face. The driver groaned softly and Robert E. literally stepped back in surprise. He nodded in approval to himself as he noticed the driver was wearing her seatbelt while at the same time noting the empty space where the windshield used to be. "Thank God for small miracles." He whistled through his teeth.

As if on cue, the driver slowly sat back, looking around warily. She first took notice of the pile of shattered glass in her lap and the lack of a windshield before her. She had a deep gash across her right brow and had blood actively falling from her nose. Trying to focus her eyes and get her bearing, the driver started cursing under her breath. She was unaware of anybody standing outside. "Dang it all." She mumbled. "Brand new truck. I should've stayed in Iraq!" She inventoried herself from head to toe, cautiously and systematically testing each limb. Everything seemed to be working fine, despite all the blood.

"A woman after my own heart." Robert E. as he instinctively reached into his pocket for a clean handkerchief. She was conscious, breathing and moving so his immediate concerns were quickly put to rest.

"You broke anywhere?" He asked as the woman attempted to unbuckle her seat-belt. "Lady, maybe you ought not to be flappin' around just yet."

The driver jumped, startled by the sound of his voice. Robert E. offered the handkerchief which she accepted gratefully. She looked warily at the bearded figure clad in Carharts and immediately took notice of the diamond stud earrings he was wearing in both ears and the small gold hoop in his left. Despite the black knit cap pulled snugly to his brows, she noted he appeared to be bald as well. Great. My Good Samaritan is Mr. Clean, she thought to herself. And what kind of guy carried handkerchiefs these days? Despite the first impressions, there was an odd air of familiarity about the fellow that she couldn't immediately place.

"I don't think so. I'm fine." She weakly attempted to open her door. "It's stuck." She started pushing at the door harder, making faces as her attempts went in vain. "I can't find my phone. I'm late. I need to call-" She was still trying to push the door with one hand and hold the handkerchief over her eye with the other. She hadn't realized her nose was bleeding as well. Robert E. had hung back, quietly observing, aware she was probably in shock.

"Hold on a minute. Let me help you before you hurt yourself."

Robert E. yanked the handle from the outside, successfully pulling the door open wide. He reached in to help her unbuckle the seat belt.

"You don't look like fine." Robert E. commented as he helped her out of the cab. "You rolled your truck and in case you hadn't noticed Sweetheart, you've hit your head, too; hard. See this hole? It used to be your window. And that one? Used to be your windshield. That little parachute piece of cloth in front of you? That used to be the airbag. Besides the nice gash over the top of your eye, you got a nose, probably broken by the way, that's bleeding, too." He gently steered her toward the tailgate, which had fallen open as the truck landed at the bottom of the hill. "Too bad, too. Looked like a nice ride."

The sense of urgency Robert E. had at the top of the hill wasn't as pressing once he'd assessed the situation. It had been less than five minutes between the time he watched the truck slide over the embankment to the time he found himself jumping after it but never the less, despite the fact that the driver was alert, walking and talking, he still felt the need to call for an ambulance. His phone was up in his truck and Robert E. didn't want to leave the driver alone. He'd heard too many stories about walking wounded.

"Come on. Sit down." Robert E. commanded gently as he helped the woman around to the battered tailgate. "Thing is, my truck's at the top of that bank you just rolled yours over. I have to run up there to get my phone." He waved vaguely to the roadway above them. "Stay right there. Don't move. I'll be right back." He briefly thought about helping her up the steep embankment to the warm, dry cab of his own truck but quickly dismissed the idea. She looks okay enough. A few more minutes out here ain't gonna hurt her any worse, he'd decided. Even so, he removed his Carhart coat and placed it over her shoulders. "Stay here. I'll be right back."

"Woof." She replied sarcastically but with a thankful smile. Emily watched as Mr. Clean climbed his way effortlessly up the embankment and then studied the scene before her, surveying the severity of damage. Gingerly, she dabbed at her nose. "Oh yeah, it's broke." Not for the first time in her life, Emily Nichols shook her head slowly back and forth, wishing literally that she had turned left instead of right.

She watched as her Good Samaritan reappeared at the roadside, sliding down the hill next to the path of freshly turned dirt her truck had turned over when it rolled. She marveled silently how she hadn't killed herself plowing down the embankment.

Either Mr. Clean hadn't caught the sarcasm in her voice or he didn't care because he made no mention of it when he returned.

"You need me to call anybody for you?" He asked automatically, controlling his breathing almost to the point of pain as he handed her his phone. "I've already called the sheriff's patrol and an ambulance." At that precise moment, Robert E. vowed to quit smoking, not wanting to let on how winded he really was from running up the hill. This was probably her husbands' truck anyway. He thought of the emblem in place on the back window. Marine.

"Not unless you know the number to Triple A or the local garage." She looked for her purse. "You wouldn't happen to have a cigarette on you, would you?"

"As a matter of fact, I do." Robert E. paused as he answered her.

"What? Have a cigarette or know the number to the local garage?"

"Both actually." He replied looking at her first without expression then did a double-take. He looked at her closely. No. Could it really be?

With the faintest hint of amusement to her expression, the driver raised a bleeding brow warily in his direction. She winced with the pain and automatically reached to touch her head. Her vision wasn't clear at the moment but she wasn't about to let this guy know that. "Guess I should call the boss man and tell him I'm probably not coming in today." She attempted a skeptical smile.

Robert E. was instantly intrigued with the woman sitting on the tailgate before him. It'd been years. Her unrestrained character immediately enamored itself to him. She cursed, was sarcastic, apparently smoked, yet still seemed to have a sense of humor; each good qualities unto themselves as far as he was concerned. She wasn't in too rough of shape, either for having just rolled a truck over a bank. He lit a cigarette and handed it to her. "Here" He finally got a closer look at the disheveled, battered and bruised woman sitting before him.

"Emily Nichols." He stated simply. Sure enough.

"Thanks." With visibly trembling hands, she accepted the Marlboro from his outstretched hand. She'd barely inhaled the first drag before she started coughing, gasping for fresh air. Robert E. quickly reclaimed the cigarette. He'd already tossed one good cigarette that morning and wasn't about to let another go to waste.

"Still don't smoke, do you?" Immediately commandeering the lit cigarette, he inhaled deeply, savoring the smoke filling his lungs. "Shouldn't have given up as quickly as you did. Second drag doesn't burn as much." She was still in a daze, not realizing who he was. It'd been several years since they'd met in Oklahoma. They'd both changed appearance enough to not instantly recognize one another, never mind the fact that she had just rolled her truck over an embankment. It wasn't as if Robert E. had expected to run into the likes of Emily Nichols that particular morning, either, but yet here they were.

"You didn't have to call any ambulance. I'm pretty sure I'm okay. I need a tow truck more than I need an ambulance."

He had a slightly bemused look on his face. "I didn't have to stop either. Why don't you let the paramedics check you out before being sure?" Robert E. felt like he should have been doing more, doing something to help other than just standing around and talking. He realized he'd already done all he could do and was now simply waiting for the ambulance and troopers to show up. His rush of adrenalin was wearing off.

She shook her head, apparently still unaware of who he was. "You're right. I don't smoke. This was my first wreck. I figured lighting up was the way to go." She continued nervously. "I get back home and it snows. I mean, it snows like this here how often? And what's the first thing I do? Wreck my truck. I've not been home a month and, well now I'm late."

"Yep." Robert E. commented nonchalantly. "Could've been worse. Bein' late for work should be the least of your concerns. I mean late beats dead, right?" Robert E. flipped the half-finished cigarette from his fingertips. "Insurance'll take care of all this." He gestured to the truck. She wasn't looking or sounding as gung-ho as she was when he'd run up to what was left of her truck just a few minutes ago. Still not hearing any telltale sirens of the ambulance, Robert E. grew stern and became more concerned. "You have insurance, right?"

She gave him a contemptuous look. "Of course I have insurance."

Robert E. nodded. "You sure you're okay? How many fingers am I holding up?" He was a construction foreman, not a paramedic.

She had closed her eyes, taking slow, deliberate breathes. "All of them, and yes. I'm fine. Just trying to get my bearing. Feeling a little woozy is all."

"Ambulance should be here soon. Maybe you should get back up in the cab and sit back until they get here." Robert E. gently suggested. He didn't know what else to do, feeling like he still hadn't done enough.

"Lighten up. You've already moved me around and I'm fine, see?" She waved her hands and kicked her feet a little. "Except for my nose maybe. Just relax Mr. Good Samaritan. I was wearing my seat belt, you know. You didn't sever my spine or anything." Emily tried to lighten the moment. "I didn't catch your name, by the way." She wanted to be sure she knew who to thank after all was said and done.

"Wow. You really must've hit your head hard. You don't recognize me? It's Robert, I mean Bob Elliott but people just call me Robert E.-"

"Nice." She interrupted. "Like Cher and Madonna, only with an initial. Does the 'E' actually stand for something or is your last name simply the letter E?" Emily's teeth were chattering. She still hadn't realized that he knew who she was. Her mind was processing a thousand things at once, never mind the fact she literally wasn't seeing things very clearly at the moment.

"Both." Robert E. adjusted the Carhart jacket he had placed around her shoulders. Now he was getting nervous. As he reached for his phone to place another call, he finally heard the faint sound of sirens in the distance.

"Mr. E. Pleased to make your acquaintance, circumstances notwithstanding. I'm Wilhelmina Nichols, United States Marine. You may call me Emily." The initial shock of rolling her truck was wearing off and Emily was now feeling the full effects of being tossed around the inside of the cab to the extent that her seat belt had allowed.

"Like I was saying, let's not dismiss the ambulance idea too soon." Robert E. sternly took charge of the situation, speaking kindly but with concern.

She did a double-take and looked at him sharply. "Oh my..." Emily spoke slowly. "Mr. E.? Robert E.? Bob Elliot?

You, it can't be. Not, I mean, wow. I thought you were still in-"

"Yep. It's really me. Only it's just plain Robert E. now, thank-you." He grinned as he breathed an audible sigh of relief. "And no, we finished Alaska just before the cold-snap really hit. I'd heard your unit was back. Saw it on TV actually, but I didn't expect that I'd be catching up with you like this."

That was then.

CHAPTER 13

THE DAY UPON HIM

Present Day

The morning dawned different for Robert E. He couldn't put a finger on it but he awoke from another restless night still hungry for uncomplicated recollection; not the reflective sort like when he used to sit with his folks and talk about the good old days. Neither was it like times he'd spend reminiscing with his brothers about the Saturdays they all spent working in the barn or remembering times when Cousin So-and-So rode sled Devil-may-care from the top of their mountain and didn't make it all the way across the creek below. No, there was a yearning that morning for something more, a longing for more than how things used to be.

"Mid-life crisis? Nostalgia? Take your pick, old boy." He grinned. "You and those ten-dollar words, Emily." Robert E. closed his eyes, fondly reflecting the selected memories he had of her that never let him rest. As long as he didn't open his eyes, he was somewhere back in time, in a safe place where everything was good. The best times of his life were mostly memories now. He took a slow, purposeful sip of coffee from the cracked mug in his hands, instantly remembering the day Mama had bought the original set from the old department store that used to sit up across the tracks. Though the store was long gone, those old mugs still remained. Only one had ever been broke through all the years and kids and now instead of a service for eight, seven well-used cups now claimed space in the cupboard over the sink. He wondered how many sets of the diamond-patterned, pearl glazed mugs that old department store actually sold that year.

"For Pete's sake." He muttered aloud to himself. "Why does my mind get hooked on such off the wall stuff?" He'd lost count of the number of times his mind had wandered off track over the years. Robert E. stood up and took a close look around the room, his eyes sweeping from the dining room windows to the picture window in the living room. "Wow." Robert E. said softly to the room. "If these walls could talk."

The familiarity of his parents' home was one comfort he was especially appreciative of at the moment. The custommade Amish dining room table with eight high-back chairs and matching buffet had been part of the rooms' decor for as long as he could remember. Mama even still got down on her hands and knees to scrub the hardwood floors once a week (she never allowed dust to settle anywhere) and there was always the subtle scent of apple pie that somehow wafted continuously year round reminding Robert E. of his formerly favorite time of year. Despite having came and went several times over the years, this was one place he knew he could always come back to and everything would be all right. It was still home to him.

The undersized, cushioned bench he was standing next to was one he'd built for his mom as a Mother's Day gift years ago. Robert E. smiled as he reached out to touch the arm. Though it was covered with all the nicks and chips that over forty years could give it and now sat a little lop-sided, his mother still adored it. The bench didn't match a stick of furniture in the entire house but Anna Elliott insisted it stay out in the open for everybody to see. For Robert E., this was home. Though his life had changed exponentially in a relatively short span of time, he'd always been able to come back. He'd felt like that with Emily, cozy and comfortable. She was always there to come home to.

"This'll all change too someday, I'm sure." Deep sigh this time. "The folks ain't getting' any younger." Robert E. purposely studied the old coffee cup, breathing in the steam. He stared at the red, cedar box for a long while, shaking his head slowly as he mustered the necessary nerve to finally do what he had been putting off for so long.

Robert E. eased himself down to the floor and pulled the box protectively to his side. Reluctantly sliding the lid back, the first thing he removed was the small, red drawstring bag containing her dog tags. He studied it for several minutes before next carefully removing the triangle-shaped mahogany flag case, gently placing it up on the bench behind him. As he set the flag along side of the red velveteen bag, he paused and stared some more. Every memory he harbored from that day immediately collected at the front of his mind. No amount of time was going to erase any of it, not completely. Closing his eyes, Robert E. sat patiently, as if waiting for a commercial break to interrupt his thoughts.

At first, he tackled the process reluctantly, methodically spreading the contents of the box across the floor before him in an organized manner. If this was all he had left, he wanted to savor each moment, make every memory last. He pulled out stacks of letters, letters he had written to her while she was deployed. Holding one bundle against his cheek, he caught the soft smell of her perfume. Mingling with that delicate scent was the weak smell of smoke. He'd never noticed it when he first read them, thinking now it must've had to do with the fact that there were dozens of letters tied together. Predictably, anxiously, he finally grew impatient and gently flipped the box onto its end. Only expecting more bundles of old photos and ribbon-bound letters to fall from the box, Robert E. was taken aback when a small journal thumped to the floor in a sprinkling of gritty, brown sand.

"Well what do you know? My own little piece of Iraq." He thought bitterly.

With each item he removed from the box, waves of memories crashed over him. Words echoed faintly, almost hauntingly as completely random thoughts swirled through his head and for a moment, he was standing beside her flag-draped coffin surrounded by unfamiliar faces of soldiers in uniform.

"Robert Anthony Elliott, I present this flag to you on behalf of our nation and the United States Marines. I am sorry for your loss." Six little words.

"Fair winds and following seas, sir." Another Marine offered a sharp salute.

Robert E. wasn't sure what that meant; fair winds and following seas. He couldn't think of a response. Not realizing he'd been holding his breath, Robert E. let it out in a slow rush and offered simply, "Semper Fi, Marine" as he did his best to return the salute he'd been given.

He remembered watching people before him, his mind wandering. Emily had once asked him a question that, at the time he thought rather peculiar.

"Robert E. If something were to happen to me while I was over there, would you make sure you'd never let any of our kids forget me? Would you tell them all about me? That's the thing that bothers me most. If I die before any of my children-"

Uncomfortable with having to answer that caliber of question, Robert E. side-stepped the question, quickly interrupting her. "Of course. Why would you think otherwise?"

One by one, other people, and more Marines slowly filed past. Robert E. figured as far as the other Marines were concerned, it was more out of respect and duty than the fact that they had actually known Emily. He knew he'd likely never see or hear from any of them again. A person's existence seemed to vanish too soon after they died and hardly anybody remembered the survivors. Robert E. didn't know who the majority of the people were anyway, just folks who'd known Emily pausing to pay final respects. At the time, Robert E. thought most of those who'd came to 'pay respects' came more for curiosity's sake, as if to see if Emily the Marine was really dead. Some seemed visibly disappointed that it was a closed-casket service. He went back to wondering how many fellow Marines from that particular day had thought about Emily since? These were part of the never-ending feelings leftover from when she died, part of some very painful memories that he'd never shaken loose; memories he did not particularly care to have.

In the weeks and months following Emily's death, Robert E. slowly grew to understand that his perception of the nightmare was completely off the mark. He was left a grieving widower; she'd gotten the easy part. She didn't have to deal with the reminders, the awkward conversations or hushed tones when she walked into a room. He was the one left behind, the one who had to constantly explain, maintain the stiff upper lip because men weren't supposed to be emotional. He was the one who had to explain to their only son why Mom wasn't coming home.

For awhile, he led an almost exhaustive existence. Of course, Robert E. knew he was wrong for thinking it in the first place, but after awhile, he didn't have to worry about those things anymore. People quit asking how he was doing because they quit stopping by, period. Life had returned to normal for all of them the moment they left the cemetery. They had nothing left to say and they didn't want to be reminded. Robert E. was the one left wishing for one more day, one more chance to say the things he'd never had chance to tell her.

"That's how it goes, I suppose." Robert E. let a single, hesitant tear fall to the floor. He stared hard at the journal before finally picking it up. "Well how 'bout that?" He exclaimed softly. "Always were full of surprises. Must've been stuck in one of the bundles I haven't gone through yet." For a brief moment, Robert E. was sorry he'd started going through her keepsakes.

She had stored numerous other mementos and souvenirs in the cedar box besides the pictures, letters, and journal. Emily had placed one of their wedding invitations inside along with a few stray pages of leftover Marine stationary. There were various military commendations, and more recent, the medals which Robert E. had placed alongside assorted letters of condolence. There were more difficult to understand items inside which he couldn't explain, like a little white jewelers box full of dried leaves labeled 'That Poinsettia Plant' and an heirloom Zippo lighter with gold-inlay. Emily didn't even smoke. Sitting atop the entire collection had been the glass fronted mahogany box containing her flag. That cedar box was a virtual time capsule, reminding Robert E. all too well of the past as well as the future, a future where the only thing he knew for certain was that she wasn't in it. Today, the cedar box seemed to be saying, "The journey is over."

It'd been nearly two years since Robert E. last opened it, completing the task he decided he had to accomplish that morning. Not a day had gone by when he didn't think of her. Time was supposed to make his loss an easier cross to bare, to accept, was supposed to heal all the wounds. It hadn't. The pain was still there, just as fresh. Time hadn't even begun to heal. Though several years had passed since her death, there were still times when that empty space loomed especially large.

Robert E. knew opening that box was going to release some very overpowering memories of her life, of their lives together. The red, cedar box had been sitting in wait under his bed, not having been disturbed since the day Robert E and LB moved in with his folks. He'd kept it within arms' reach though and every night before falling asleep, he'd reach under the bed to lay his hand on it, reassuring himself it was still there. It was Robert E.'s last connection to her, a reason why he kept putting off what he knew he needed to do. At first, as occasions warranted, he'd added things to the box just as he thought Emily would have continued doing. Those occasions grew less frequent as time continued to pass by but more than once, just knowing the box was there; holding all those memories within arm's reach helped him through more than a few nights.

Despite being financially capable of keeping the home they had built together, it proved too much to bear walking into a house every night that reminded him of what he'd lost. The little two-story cottage eventually turned into a place where he'd periodically attempt to drown his sorrows, to escape from reality. He'd lost Emily too many times before finally asking her to marry him and now there was no way to bring her back. Just in time for the real estate bust that hit the entire nation, Robert E. had finally put the house up for sale. Secretly, he was glad it'd taken such a long time to sell because it had afforded him a private place to go, to be alone and remember her. It was the place that before it sold, where he had almost decided to end it all. He had mixed feelings the day he turned the key over to the new owner, but as he packed up the last pieces of furniture, he realized it was for the best, something he had to do. In all reality, Robert E. knew that the sale of the little house had probably saved his life.

Rain fell steadily against the panes of aged, lead-base painted windows still in place in the corner of his parent's dining room as little wisps of smoke from the pipe on the ancient wood stove transported him further back in time. His folks had all the old windows in the house replaced with fancy, new energy-efficient vinyl ones except, to his father's overly exaggerated dismay, for the ones in the dining room. Robert E. remembered his mothers' winning argument.

"I don't want to replace all of them, Jon." Anna Elliott insisted. "Those old windows are part of why we bought this house in the first place, part of its charm. It's not as if we need worry about the kids chewing on the window-sills." She'd laughed. "Let's keep the original decor and leave the dining room alone. Nobody will notice. And so what if they do? Honestly, who's going to come into our house and tell us what they think is wrong with it? We can still buy the replacements but we'll store them in the garage, you know in case we change our minds later." Mama had never changed her mind. The replacements were still stored out in the garage.

Focusing on the task at hand, Robert E. ignored the journal and picked up a ribbon-bound bundle, carefully untied it and started to slowly sort through the letters. There were dozens of them. She'd kept every one he'd ever written. They weren't in haphazard lots, either. As was Emily's meticulous style, every letter was in chronological order, by day, by month, by year. Separate bundles; his letters to her, her letters to him; all together, all in order. Emily had even gone as far as tying the bundles in pink or blue ribbons depending on who wrote them.

"I'd wondered where these had gotten off to." He smiled at her perfectionism. Every envelope was stacked with the return address in the upper left corner, no ragged flaps to be found. Every one had been neatly cut open on the right hand side.

"I've put them in a safe place," She'd told him "for prosperity's sake. When the time is right, you'll find them easily enough. I promise."

For no reason in particular, Robert E. remembered and finally understood what at the time had seemed such a trivial matter. One morning over breakfast years ago, Emily had read out loud a bit of philosophical journalism, something that had really upset her. Somebody had published something about how there was a place for everyone in this world as long as one was alive but when a person ceased to exist, then their place among the living did as well. Robert E. remembered Emily close to tears when she'd exclaimed from out of the blue, "Not true." She then went on to explain that Marine or not, there were just some things people shouldn't do.

"Like 'never forget'. I know it sounds all gung-ho and maybe a little Jar-headed but," Emily had cast a sidelong glance at Robert E. who merely smiled in response, acknowledging the jab he had taken at their first reunion "-if everybody practiced in their life what Marines are trained to do regarding the way of life in the Corps in general, there'd be a lot less problems with the world. Values, Robert E. Values. Everybody has to have a set of values to stand for. People don't pass down tradition or morals anymore. People don't think they have to be accountable for their own actions. For the longest time I didn't understand all the ritual and routine associated with the Marines. I mean, every branch of the military has its traditions and some might say quirks, but being a Marine? It's meant being intense with every detail, every tradition. It's someone I have become. You know, when my unit started taking heavy casualties on a daily basis, I saw unthinkable things. Wasn't in a combat position, no but what I saw," She paused "- it wasn't just ambushes or air strikes we had to be concerned with. There were many ways that people, insurgents invented to take people out, to kill Americans. Marketplaces, bazaars, funerals, it didn't matter. Anywhere people would gather together was fair game. I saw Iraqi authorities shoot at this one guy and watched him literally explode; no pieces to pick up. And just when I thought I saw everything, here came the next bunch of suicide bombers pirating fuel tankers, hiding explosives in their own body cavities, and I didn't see this but heard about donkey suicide bombers…" Emily paused dramatically. "Donkeys, Robert E. I imagine somewhere somebody's epitaph reads 'death by donkey.' "

Robert E. had no idea. She wasn't supposed to be seeing any of that, at least not in his mind, not in that detail. He'd read about horrors of Viet Nam and the tactics used against troops there but he didn't think Emily was supposed to have to worry about that stuff in Iraq.

"If all of that isn't enough to think about, they've got women stepping up to be suicide bombers now. A bunch of

Shiites in Baghdad were killed not long ago. And you want to know the worst thing? There were reports that the bombers in that attack were mentally retarded women. Those poor women had Down's syndrome and no idea what was going on, no competence to pull off that sort of thing. Can you imagine?"

Robert E. didn't know what to say. He didn't want to try imagining the things she described.

"Leave no man behind, extremely serious stuff. You know, you can pretty much always tell a Marine, even in civvies." He thought back to their reunion in Oklahoma. She was right. Even if he hadn't already had known she was a Marine, he'd have speculated she was at least in some branch of the military at least just for how she carried herself when she walked across the parking lot that morning.

It wasn't such a trivial thing after all, Robert E. thought to himself. "It's all about the discipline." Robert E. wasn't sure anymore that she was wrong about any of that.

Too poignant, too sentimental, too feeling, too headstrong. Each of these was things said by many who knew nothing about her before she ever went through boot camp. She became a Marine, but was still an artist at heart and the point was, after all, to actually be each of those things in the first place. He got that. It was part of the more engaging qualities she possessed, her sentimentality. It was ultimately because of her that they had reunited in the first place; both times. She didn't have to agree to meet in Oklahoma.

"No philosopher and hardly any novelist has ever managed to explain what that weird stuff, human consciousness, is really made of." She'd continued reading to him. "Natural events; things that happen through chance and circumstance and in enormously complex ways." She'd dropped the paper in her lap and looked thoughtfully out the window. Robert E.

sensed she was waiting for his response, or in the very least, an acknowledgement to her comment. He stopped what he was doing and waited, giving her his full attention.

"Do you believe our finding each other again was like that? Was it circumstance or chance?" Not expecting him to reply, she picked the paper up to continue.

"Both," He'd interrupted surprisingly. "-definitely both." He replied without offering any more comment and studied her face as she turned thoughtful again. He knew she had more to say and waited patiently. He remembered the last time he'd failed to answer her without his full attention. It was after Oklahoma. She'd purposely avoided telling him about any additional military obligations and he couldn't help but think he probably would've had more time than he eventually got if he'd only been a little more attentive.

Though he was like many people and was blissfully unaware of any major military conflicts going on at the time, Robert E. had been surprised when he'd found out Emily had not returned to Mena after their reunion in Oklahoma. Their meeting had been just after the horrifying events of September 11 and he'd assumed that when they'd parted ways on the Interstate that morning, she was headed back home, that he'd be able to get back in touch his next time through. He'd made good on the phone calls and letter attempts a few times but apparently his efforts weren't enough. When he'd returned, she was nowhere to be found. Of course, Mrs. Rainey told him Emily had been deployed but nobody knew when she'd be back.

"I didn't know how I was going to do it at the time. I waited too long the first time and wasn't going to lose you again. That time, I believed more in Fate than circumstance." It was she who called him. "I wanted to talk to you one more time."

She'd waited for his response. As he sat in silence, waiting for her to continue, Robert E. nodded his slow, Robert E. nod to himself, imagining her expression.

"I've wanted to make all of my moments, Robert E. I've never been satisfied with sitting around waiting to see what was going to happen next. I've always tried minimizing my regrets. I felt like I had an obligation, especially after what's happened in New York and Washington. I'm going back." She spoke so softly that he almost didn't hear what she'd said.

"Em, remember what you said about that? About minimizing the regrets? About turning moments of your life into exactly what you wanted them to be?" Robert E. figured he didn't have anything to lose so he poured his heart out. As he told her everything, Emily never interrupted. There had always been many thoughts but now many new questions running through her mind as well.

"Aren't you going to say anything?" He asked.

Taking a moment to compose herself before commenting, Emily at last responded in her characteristically quiet manner.

"I am who I am, Robert E. Don't try figuring me out now." She'd paused, thinking carefully before telling him what she had to say next. "I have a few days if, well if you wanted to see me before I have to leave-"

That was all she had to say. Robert E. managed the next flight back to Arkansas. He thought it was going to be simple, easy to pick up where they'd left off. It wasn't. Theirs was a tale certainly befitting of once upon a time but it was entirely up to Fate if there would be any happily ever after. Neither of them had any idea of what lay around the corner.

CHAPTER 14

LEFT WONDERING

Robert E. had become so caught up in replaying old memories that he knew he wouldn't be going anywhere that morning. It was something that'd started with relative infrequency; unexpected feelings that he couldn't place. There had been a sudden darkness first, then a fog he couldn't see through, couldn't shake. Even before he sold the house, Robert E. felt himself slipping a little each day into an unfamiliar place yet with almost a sense of having been there before. It was dread between being afraid he would forget Emily completely and fearing he would never again feel for anyone the feelings he had for her. He found himself continuously searching for answers but never finding the ones he wanted.

He couldn't explain it but he felt as if the connection still existed between him and Emily. It wasn't the fact that they'd had a child that made Robert E. feel that way. LB was a remarkable little boy, a Godsend. It was something else. Sorting through the photographs and souvenirs in the cedar box made him think of unfinished business, business he could not identify. Each day that passed took him further and further from what he thought he remembered. The walls around him were slowly disintegrating but he couldn't do anything about it. Each night, he attempted sleep with the dread of another night alone, waiting for what walls were left standing to crumble down around him.

Robert E. wouldn't admit he was still having problems. He was too focused on maintaining the life he had with Emily for their son's sake, at least that's what he told himself. He knew he was preoccupied with her even now. His agitation and lack of focus on job sites was a matter of great discussion among his crews and was starting to cause problems. There'd been a few incidents that could've easily led to more serious catastrophes. He remembered one incident witnessed by his foreman and good friend, Paul Dooley.

Robert E. had returned to work immediately after Emily died more to get his mind off the fact that she was really gone than for the need to make money. He and Paul were framing an addition when, not for the first time after Emily's death, Robert E.'s hammer squarely met the index finger on his left hand. Howling in unexaggerated pain, he'd automatically flung the hammer, narrowly missing the head of an electrician innocently at work across the site.

Paul calmly stopped hammering and looked at Robert E., studying his face for a moment. He knew his friend clearly wasn't back to 100%, hadn't been since the day his wife died. "Jus' my opinion mate, but uh, maybe you should really take some time off. I mean, really take some time. You're not ready to be out here yet."

"Maybe you need to mind your own business Dools. I'm fine." Though Robert E. hated to admit it, Paul was probably right.

"Jus' me sayin', mate." Paul hadn't taken the remark personally. He was well aware of the circumstances under which Robert E. had lost his wife, how he'd unexpectedly became a single parent. Robert E. had every right to be affected by his loss but no right to jeopardize the safety of his crew. Though he was physically there, on time every time, his mind wasn't totally on the job and nobody needed the potential consequences of that.

Robert E. stared at Paul in silence. He was right. Paul was looking out for the guys under him, doing what a good foreman should be doing. He never minced words, always telling things as he saw them, even to the bosses. That was one of the qualities Robert E. had liked about the Aussie from the start. When Paul Dooley was on the job, nobody ever got hurt.

"Paul, I'm sorry man. I'm not-"

"No worries mate. I know." Paul shrugged his shoulders and went back to work as if nothing had happened. Left with his own thoughts, he worried about his boss. Robert E. had taken the news of Emily's death especially hard and it was obvious the man still had not gotten a grip on things. "But how do you tell a man he needs professional help?" Paul wondered to himself. As fearless and outspoken as he was, he knew some things were better left unsaid. Paul wondered how long before Robert E. would have a total breakdown. He didn't want to see that happen to his friend.

Despite all the outward signs, Robert E. continued to resist the fact that he really did need help. He didn't want to give anybody excuse to pity him or think he was weak.

"I'm not some crack-pot, you know. I just need a little more time, is all." At least that's what he'd convinced himself. There wasn't anything wrong with him. He was still grieving the loss of his wife, sure; nothing wrong with that. He simply wasn't ready to own up to the fact that he was having any problems dealing with her death.

While it was happening, Robert E. wasn't aware. It was only after people quit trying to approach him, quit calling him, that Robert E. realized how he'd alienated so many. Paul Dooley was the only one who'd continued to call, but even his calls weren't as frequent as they'd once been. Robert E. couldn't blame anyone but himself. He didn't know how to handle his life once Emily was no longer physically a part of it.

It was appropriate how almost overnight the weather had finally taken its' expected turn into autumn. It was as if yesterday summer had officially ended and fall began. According to the calendar, that really was the case. Leaves had already started turning color and the days were steadily waning. It wouldn't be long before the sound of chainsaws and smell of burning leaves would fill the air. In the mornings, fog hung suspended at the top of the mountain, slowly settling across the grown-over fields that had once constituted pastures. By noon, the fog disappeared and the skies turned a brilliant, sapphire blue.

Robert E. thoughtfully continued his recollection and soon his mind began playing on an event he and Emily had attended early in their marriage. She'd wanted to see a real play in a real theater, actually begging Robert E. to 'have some culture at least once' in his life.

"If you go this one time, I'll never ask again. I promise."

So they went. It was a black tie affair complete with black bow ties but Robert E. had refused to wear the preppy, black twill pants that Emily'd bought for the occasion, opting instead for a comfortable pair of new jeans and a favorite pair of well-worn cowboy boots. It was his little way of letting her believe that despite the fact she'd persuaded him into going, he was still in charge. (That's what she let him think, anyway.)

"If they don't like the way I look Em, well then I'm not sorry." He wasn't about to let her know it but he was actually a little nervous.

Robert E. remembered that night plainly. Emily hadn't fussed too badly; she had been delighted that he'd agreed to go in the first place. Em was true to her word too, never asking him to another formal event and never bringing up theater show again. Besides, he'd done everything she had asked. He never actually told her, but he rather enjoyed the play. He didn't exactly go in suit and tie (and as it turned out, neither did a handful of other men) but it wasn't as stifling of an experience as he thought it was going to be.

"Now, I get to ask something of you just once." He teased. Emily winced. She had a feeling she already knew what he was about to ask.

"Yes?" She asked cautiously.

"Would you consider going to one pro-game at the Dome? In Louisiana" He knew full well there was no way she'd set foot into any football stadium, much less purposely fly south to do it.

"Rob-" Emily looked at him with almost pleading eyes.

"Okay, okay." He held up his hands in mock defense. "Then would you care if I went?" He'd interrupted sheepishly. "One game? With the guys?"

He'd gone to New Orleans with his buddies and true to his word, never asked her to attend, much less consider, another professional sporting event. That was how life went between the two of them, and it worked wonderfully. Truth be told, he'd always wanted to go to a Broadway-type show, he just didn't know what he wanted to see or how to make reservations. He definitely had no idea what to wear but wasn't about to let

Emily know all of that. That was why he wasn't all broken up about her not wanting to go to a pro game. He knew she hated professional sports. He'd already learned that there were more worthy battles to fight.

Before reading from the journal he held in his hands, Robert E. admired the ornate script, the perfect letters; the words from her hand. Despite all the technology of the current century, Emily always found the time for handwritten entries in her journals.

Tonight was just like that Williams' play that I finally talked Robert E. into going to see. "Keeping with the atmosphere of some long lost memory, the lights were dim. It wasn't like we were there hearing things we thought we should have heard but more like we were somewhere else entirely, thinking of something else and all this was in the background..."

Some would call it déjà vu maybe; perhaps. I don't know. Last night when Robert E. came in from work, I just sat there thinking how lucky we were to have found each other again. Everything has happened for us probably for reasons we'll never know, but this is my life now and I can't describe how glad I am that he's finally in it for good. I don't know what I'd ever do without Robert E.

At first he hadn't let anything show. He was a man and real men weren't in the habit of wearing their emotions on their sleeve. He never talked about it, never took any of the counseling that was only eventually offered, never let anybody see him sorting through her things. Grief-work. That's what people called it. To Robert E. it was personal, something he had to work through on his own terms. Though he was proud that his wife had chosen the military as a career, that she had gained her commission such as she did, he felt odd explaining himself, that it was his wife who was the active duty Marine in the family, that he wasn't even a veteran. It wasn't as if he were opposed to the idea of women in the military, he was just never interested in being part of the 'Semper Fi' culture himself. Besides, back in the day when he probably should have thought about enlisting, he was busy working on getting the baseball scholarship that eventually earned him the degree he needed to get out of Arkansas. The draft was discontinued in 1973 and because of that, Robert E. was part of the all-volunteer generation required by law to register with Selective Service. He wasn't one who wanted to 'be all that you could be,' wasn't interested in being part of 'the few or the proud' club or even one of the guys 'aiming high' as far as a career in the military went. His folks weren't particularly concerned one way or the other about the idea of life in the military either. His father Jon was a Korean War vet, a paratrooper with the 82nd Airborne. (Try convincing him Korea was 'just a conflict'.) His mother'd lost a brother to Viet Nam and wasn't keen of the possibilities of losing any of her sons to the military. As small as his school was, there were already several members from a graduating class behind him in the ground because of what was going on in Iraq and Afghanistan, two guys that were somebody's sons, somebody's fathers. Now there was somebody's wife, somebody's mother who had been laid to rest as well.

He'd found it a few weeks before the move, a rogue letter folded neatly into thirds sitting harmlessly enough beneath a stack of California king sheets. (He'd always marveled how at 5'5 she could fold those things without a single corner touching the floor.) Finding the note was a pleasant surprise to say the least, coming at a time when he needed it most.

Robert E. ordinarily spent the majority of the last ninety days of the year trying to shake impossibilities and memories from his mind. It was never easy. Then there it was; the unexpected letter.

"It's a sign. It must be another sign."

Dear Robert E.

I don't know what you'll think when you find this letter but I felt like leaving you a little surprise to find. You know, like when you reach into an old coat pocket and find money? Anyway, there isn't anything I haven't already told you, but just thought it'd be fun to leave you a few notes.

It's kind of like you and I, you know? Finding a surprise one day from out of the blue? Your phone call brought us back together even after all the time that had passed. Robert E., not a single day that goes by that I don't think about all the twists of fate, all the coincidences. It's not all been by chance, has it? There's been something more at work here than what either one of us has been able to see. It's always been that way Robert E. How was it that we were both placed upon this Earth at the same time to experience this together? I don't even know what 'this' is, just that it's something we both've been given. It's more than Fate.

He aimed the remote into the living room, pointing it at the television looking for some acceptable, ambiguous background noise. All he found as he flipped between channels were pretty little newscasters talking about hidden agendas in the current presidential administration, reports about the latest employment crisis in America and then seemingly as in afterthought, a forcibly lighthearted reminder of the latest number of casualties of American troops.

"And now with the latest news from Iraq…"

Robert E. quickly raced through the channels. He didn't care about Iraq and he didn't need reminders glaring at him from every angle. Iraq meant only one thing to him and for the last three years he was trying to get past that. For him, that little God-forsaken country was the reason why he was a widower. It was supposed to matter to him that Emily died in service to her country? It was supposed to make him feel better that "at least she was doing what she wanted to do when she died"? Who really knew what she wanted to be doing at that exact moment? God? Well he sure let everybody down didn't he?

The next channel showed two people debating more accountability, reconciliation, reconstruction, humanitarianism and whatever other -ism and —ity they could throw into a thirty-eight second sound bite about Afghanistan and Iraq. The newscaster patriotically spewed her closing proclamation.

"United States Marines have gained the reputation they have because they refuse to quit."

"Bitch." Robert E. muttered bitterly, uncharacteristically. That perky little blond had probably never once considered a career in the military. What did she know about the Marines or any branch of the military for that matter except for what the teleprompter told her to say? He didn't need news from Iraq to remind him he needed to find his faith; reasons had already been given to him several times over. That was why he was where he was now, just looking for something to believe in.

He muttered in frustration. "Let's put out more propaganda to get America to rally behind the troops like a bunch of sheep." Robert E. briefly acknowledged the television before turning it off completely. He let out a deep sigh then laughed out loud to the room.

"It's come to this now, has it? Talking to the television?" Shaking his head to himself, Robert E. looked around the vast, open floor plan of his parents' home and studied the various knick-knacks that his mother had collected over the years, reminders of his childhood. "Who said that once you leave, you can never go back?" He smiled to himself. "I've left all this on more than one occasion and look where I'm sitting right now."

All morning as he sorted through and read the various letters, the popular hymn rang through his head like a Christmas carol in December. Problem was, it was only mid-September. No matter how hard he tried to shake it, the melody lingered, creeping from the back of his mind, "What a friend we have in Jesus."Robert E. couldn't remember the last time he'd been to church much less the last time he'd heard that particular hymn.

LB had awoke early enough to ride to church with Grandma and Grandpa so Robert E. sat by himself as he started sorting through the cedar box. He knew before he even started the task that morning that it wasn't going to be something he could start and finish in one day but it was still something he had to do. He had been putting it off for far too long.

Robert E. never realized how numerous the letters were that he and Emily had exchanged. The earliest letters bore postmarks from Fairbanks, dating back to his contractor days in Alaska. He chuckled to himself as he thought about all the times he sent new guys out to "start clearing for the foundation." With five feet of perma-frost year round, there was no way any holes were getting dug anywhere in Alaska. His brief moment of humor quickly turned solemn as he realized he had never taken her to visit any of the places he had worked in that last American Frontier.

"Always a day late, Robert E." She teased.

"And a dollar fifty short, Emily."

She'd looked at him quizzically.

"Inflation." He'd shrugged and grinned.

There were scores of photographs to account for as well, divided into neat stacks. She'd taken almost every one. He knew exactly why. "Someday you'll be glad…"

"You ask me why I take so many confounded pictures? Confounded, Robert E? Really? Someday you'll be glad I did." She'd smiled. "Remember that commercial? 'You don't take a picture, you borrow it.' Pictures are borrowed moments in time. I mean, look who's talking, right? Look at all the fine moments I've borrowed here; all the very specific moments. People will see the world through my eyes, just like you have for all these years." She ignored his puzzled expression. "Someday you'll get it, Robert E. Our meeting again wasn't strictly by chance, not even Fate. It had to do with something a little more than faith, even. Besides, people are supposed to remember, right? Not forget. And yes, I know, I know; one hundred years from now, nobody is going to care a whit about what, who, when, or why any of these were taken but you know what? I don't care that they won't care. Our kids will know," She'd emphasized the word 'our'"-and their families will know. That's all the future I can worry about today. The rest is what we make up as we go along." He now understood why she was always taking pictures. "Some people hold too tightly to the past and don't leave any room for the present. Some try to totally forget their pasts and still aren't ever able to figure out their future. That's the sad part." She had playfully snapped a picture of him that morning drinking coffee and holding the baby just for the sake of taking a picture. She'd made her point. "It's because of our pasts that we better prepare for the future."

Hard to believe LB was already going on six. Seemed like only yesterday when Emily'd told Robert E. they were expecting. "Just consider all those confounded pictures as reminders for the times you may get stuck." She offered almost prophetically. "There'll be all of these moments, these very explicit moments that I'll have captured for you personally, ready to take you back. Then, when you least expect it, they'll help push you forward."

Pictures; trademarks of a woman he knew more profoundly than even he had ever realized. They had a shared affinity for photography but this time there was something more than just the printed images on glossy card stock that struck him. Robert E. couldn't describe how, but any time he and Emily were together, he felt as if he were experiencing whatever was before them through her eyes, her mind. It wasn't a matter of simply rehashing memories over familiar photographs, either but more like watching the same channel on the television except from different rooms. It was for the same reason he always seemed to know what she was thinking before she spoke. He never felt the need to ask for elaboration. He just knew. Of course, that approach had backfired on him though as occasionally she believed he'd been disinterested or ignoring her altogether. He thought he was being a good listener- a trait she sometimes mistook for lack of interest. He never tried explaining the phenomenon, just accepted it, taking it as more insight to the touchy-feely things Emily liked to spring on him.

Then he found it.

Robert E. remembered the day he had taken it. At that moment, he couldn't explain why he'd felt especially compelled in getting that particular shot. Suddenly, none of that mattered. He knew. He just knew. It was because he'd seen it through her eyes. Tucked protectively between the bundles of letters was the picture of the old railroad trestle he'd taken during their reunion out west. The photograph wasn't actually taken in Oklahoma either but on their way down one of the scenic byways in Arkansas. How many miles had they put on that rental car in three days? He remembered traveling down the byway after leaving Branson and catching the scene as the sun was setting that evening. He'd forgotten he'd sent her a copy. Turning the picture over, he smiled as he read where Emily had added her own caption; "Our Bridge of Madison County."

"You said someday I'd be glad. Em," he sighed out loud "- today's one of those days."

In many ways, Emily had always been poles apart from other women he knew. As outgoing and extroverted as she was, Robert E. knew Emily lived in a world all her own; always had. Hers was a combination of living with morals and ethics from a previous generation, a past she wasn't even born into and the old country music she'd grown up on. There was always the music. It was more of a cultural sort of thing, really; the language of the moment, a sign of the times; just like how nobody 'dothed' or 'thoued' anymore. Even before the Corps, Emily was one who believed in Civic responsibility when many people didn't even know or perhaps had forgotten what Civic responsibility was all about.

Call it awareness of the human condition or just plain being aware, but when Emily talked, she made people feel as if they were all that mattered at that particular moment in time. When she would speak to a person, it was always with genuine interest, never forced, never phony. When she engaged an individual in a conversation, she had a way of showing, not just telling that person she meant every word she spoke. Despite all her insight, there was still a side to Emily that Robert E. had never been able to follow.

Emily was the only individual he knew who still would go out of her way to send handwritten thank-you cards or letters just for the sake of writing them. He remembered her self-confessed practice of counting of feathers in hats at church on Sundays.

"I read a story somewhere, can't remember exactly when or where or why I even read it but part of the story had a character who liked counting feathers in hats in church on Sundays. I decided I'd do it too, I mean what better place than church to count people who wore hats?" She'd grinned and laughingly punched Robert E.'s shoulder. "Remember, I always thought I had better places to be than in church. Everyone should have a story, right? I mean, everyone can create their own interesting life; the problem is that people seem intent on living theirs just like everybody else's, worrying about keeping up with some Jones or other. You can't reasonably expect that." Emily paused in thoughtful reflection.

"When I was younger, Mom used to drag all of us kids to church every Sunday. I didn't want to sit in a pew all day and always thought I had better things to do. I mean what kid wants to dress up in good clothes one more day of the week just to go listen to somebody talk about God? Especially during summer vacation? But I went. And don't get me wrong. I'm glad I did. I kept myself amused by counting the number of little old ladies who still wore hats at the big Baptist Church up town. There used to be so many that I had to figure out different categories to sort everybody into. Hats I mean, not the ladies. That would've been a whole other can of worms." She'd grinned. "My favorite group was feathers. Every week I'd wait and see how many ladies wore hats with feathers in the bands. You know, over the years the few that there were began turning into less and less. It took silly, little, naive me quite awhile to figure out why all the ladies wearing hats were slowly disappearing. I'd ignored the fact I was growing older, too. By the time I realized nothing or anybody lasts forever, Mama wasn't so insistent in any of us attending church every Sunday. You see, she was getting older herself and had decided to keep her own kind of pew."

"Her own kind of what?" Robert E. wasn't following.

"Pew. You know, as in church bench? She'd decided she didn't need to sit on any particular bench to believe in her religion just because that was everyone else in town chose to do." Emily turned thoughtful again. "Mom always told me that you can't just stand around wondering what happened in your life. You've got to make things happen. Otherwise, you're gonna step back one day and ask yourself, 'Hey? What the heck happened? It all goes back to saying life is what we make of it."

The place in time where Emily liked to exist was one where men still stood and tipped their hats when a woman entered a room or begged a lady's pardon when a curse word escaped in her presence. Chivalry Emily'd called it. It was the place in time when the women stayed home and the men went off to war. It was the same place where people actually cared about Memorial Day and Veteran's Day. No woman he could name wore a hat to church these days and no man he knew gave a rip if a woman was within earshot when a curse word slipped. A lot of the women he knew cussed and argued just as well as any man he knew. Of course he hadn't been to church for awhile. Maybe hats were in vogue again. As far as women staying at home with the children while the men went off to fight? These days, it wasn't just women and children left waving their good-byes at the airport seeing their spouses off to war. It wasn't as if Emily was jaded or ever claimed the world was really like that either. If it would have been in her power to have chosen a specific place in time to be born, then that was where she would liked to have been.

"It only takes one person to create change Robert E., just one. I'd like to be one of them, one of those who made this world a nicer place to exist for someone, even if only for a little while. I mean, you don't think Rosa Parks woke up that morning thinking she was going to change history, do you? Just one person…"

"God, Em. You succeeded in that twice; for a little while." Robert E. closed his eyes as he thought of how brief the time was that their little family had shared together. LB could barely remember her. "You were one of those people, Em. You made a huge difference in my life."

"Progress hasn't necessarily been all for the good, you know." She'd once said. "I thought long and hard about my life before deciding to try getting into a military academy and I didn't choose the Marines because I had anything to prove, either. I did it because it felt like it was where I'd fit best. You know the whole 'Semper Fi' thing? I mean, I'd considered the Army and Air Force at one point but the Marines just seemed like the best fit. I'm not knocking any of the other branches, but I'm glad I didn't go any other route. I needed to be challenged; to make sure I really wanted what I thought was right. When Daddy died, that sort of clinched it. Semper Fi, in honor of my father. It seemed the right decision to make."

"Girl, don't I know it." He thought to himself. "Semper Fi, Emily." Robert E. whispered to the empty room. He remembered…

Robert E. wasn't sure what direction the conversation was headed and patiently waited for Emily to continue.

"I feel like I need to validate myself, my decision to go back." She explained to his puzzled expression. "I've worked hard to get where I am. I mean, an officer in the Marines of all things. I didn't have anything on the outside to look forward to until you came back into my life. I've always thought about us Robert E., always thought about someday…"

Robert E. thought about one of their last conversations. Emily had started questioning her commitment to the Corps. As he continued sorting through the bundles of old letters, Robert E. finally found the one he'd been looking for. Emily felt as if she'd fulfilled a goal, a commitment, and an obligation. He had to wonder what made her change her mind.

CHAPTER 15

THE LETTER

Dear Robert E.15 August

Back again, just now getting a break. It's about as hot as I imagine it could be in Hades in August. Lucky for you then, right? That's because I decided to try writing some more of your letter to get my mind off the heat. That's how I do it, you know; write you your letters in little bursts whenever I can because Lord knows I don't get much time to just sit and write a decent one from start to finish. Besides, letters are always nice to have when you want to remember those epic moments, right? It seems over here that every day is an epic moment and music should be playing in the background nonstop. You know, like that website?

Be right back. Mortar rounds. I ha-

I'm back. Sorry 'bout the break. Now where was I? Shoot, I can't remember what I was going to tell you. Oh, mortars… Nothing unusual, at least from this end; interruptions by mortar rounds. More for me to worry about when you start getting interrupted by them over there. Ha ha, right?

I'm sure you haven't felt compelled to be riveted to the television much the past few days, (months or years) and you might think nothing new is going on in this big sandbox across the sea. Same old, same old. Right? Well, don't be too sure about that. Things are happening pretty much on a daily basis that even we don't know about until a week or two goes by then from out of the blue, we get an "Oh by the way, did you hear…"

I brought a press group through camp the other day and overheard a conversation that really struck me. I mean, everybody has a right to their opinions and all of us here are obligated to keep everybody back home informed but this press group was a different bunch. A few of them were pretty vocal in questioning why the U.S. is still here. They were respectful enough, but I could tell they had a lot on their minds.

16 August

A person has to be pretty careful about what and who she says anything to around here. You know how that book said that even the so-called 'off the record' conversations really weren't? It's true. You can't say what you really feel lest anyone anger the press or sour the public back home. When that happens, everyone has to contend with pissed off commanders so generally, it's best to keep comments and opinions to one's self.

What that reporter said the other day certainly was true enough though. He said something to the effect of how nice it would be if the United States were as concerned with the welfare of the people of our own country as we've been with Iraq. Sure, we've all thought that at one time or another, I mean, I've even said it but he was the first PR guy I've heard say it. Apparently, somebody's not too popular back in the District of Columbia?

EMILY'S ROBERT E.

17 August

"There's no such thing as free speech. You pay for everything you say." We have to be over here, although the natives are still trying to figure out why. (To tell you the truth, so am I.) It's all for the cause, that global fight against terrorism, the search for those weapons of mass destruction you probably hear about every night on the news. Might not be all in black and white (actually there's lots of gray areas) but we're supposed to be here. Just ask the last couple of Commanders-in-Chief. Deep sigh. If you ask me, it's all been in the name of greed. But then again, how brave does the Commander-in-Chief have to be to sit behind a desk and commit other people's lives to chance? He gives the orders and we just follow them. Yes sir. You bet, sir.

I know. I'm the one who wanted to be a Marine. I signed up for this. I'm not supposed to question the things I'm ordered to do, not suppose to make or publicize any opinions I might have. I totally understand that, too. But the longer we're here, the more I find myself wondering and questioning (at least to myself) what exactly we have or were supposed to have accomplished. Escorting press groups around and listening to them talk? I feel like that's all I've accomplished. I thought there was supposed to be more.

We're sitting in one of the oldest civilizations on the planet, a place I used to think of as a little piss ant country that just happened to be located over some of the largest oil reserves in the world. We've bombed the glory out of this place and they've give it right back. We've been shot at, lied to and even taken prisoners. But what have we accomplished?

18 August

Think all the way back to 2001, our Day of Infamy. That was what, ten years after the first time we were over here? This time, the actual war didn't start until 2003. By the end of that year, we found Hussein and I thought, "Good. We've finally accomplished what we've set out to do." I thought we'd be coming back home lickety-split, except guess what? We didn't. And now, how many thousands of lives has it cost to see us this far?

Robert E., I hope we never have to experience what it's like to fight all-out war in our own towns and burgs. I'm not talking World Trade Center or Washington D.C. proportions. I mean not being able to go to the grocery store because somebody might shoot you as you walk out the door type of stuff just because you were wearing the wrong clothes or somebody suspected you were talking to the wrong people. (Oh wait. We already have that, don't we? It's called Little Rock. Not funny, by the way.)

I'm living, no existing in a tent in the middle of a desert in a country full of people who have strong opinions about why we're here to begin with. We were supposedly coming to fight a war on terrorism, then we were here to help these people and well, dang it Robert E., as far as I can see, we've only made more of a mess out of things. This country is in worse shape than it was before we got here.

Snipers over here are thinking of ways to peck off troops before breakfast every morning like we wonder when this is all going to be over every night. Their days start with waking up thinking about how many people they'll get to shoot like we wake up wondering what's for chow. That's what they do, that's their job. And don't forget the rebels who know daily schedules who might let a convoy pass today, then maybe tomorrow kill one or two of us just because they can. Roadside bombs go off with such a rate that the noise isn't such a big deal anymore, it's a given. If it's quiet for too long, everybody starts wondering what's going to happen next. With all this, one might think a person would get used to all the death and dying that goes along with war. I'm telling you that's a crock. You never get used to it, any of it. Ever. People who say they do are liars. There are things worse than death and I believe I've seen some of them.

On the brighter side, let me tell you something good. In all of the endless nothingness Iraq has to offer, it has had one thing wonderful to put forward. When night falls, this place comes to life. I'm not talking about people or mortar fire or anything like that. It's something that makes me feel like I'm back home, up on the mountain by the lodge. Stars, Robert E. Who would've thought, right?

The sky; it's so dark here, so black with nothing but the curve of the earth blocking the view. I've never seen anything so beautiful. The Middle East isn't all about war and death or oil. Those little specks of light you see in the sky remind me that there are better days ahead.

19 August

What you are probably getting to see on the television isn't what's really going on over here. You're just seeing the low lights, seeing what you're supposed to see, watching the stuff that's theoretically going to whip up support to keep the troops from missing home. We pretty up for press visits, tell them what they want to hear, show them what Marines are really made of and how we get the job done. What you don't get to see are all the unemployed, homeless and flat out scared Iraqis who dart through the streets, scurrying in the alleys. That's the scary part. Sometimes we don't see them but they always see us and that's not always been a good thing.

That leaves one thing always in the back of my mind, Robert E. It only takes one shot, one bullet, one bomb and that scares me. I mean, I know...most of the stuff I worry about won't ever happen. But this is Iraq. A lot of that stuff happens every day and I do worry about it; all of the time. I have to wonder if one day something is going to happen to me.

I've thought a lot about that Robert E. What if one day I was the one? I have to think about that, being over here, you can't assume nothing couldn't happen to you, just by the virtue of this being war. What troubles me most is that if something did happen to me, would you make sure LB knew all about me? All about us and how he even came to be in our lives? Would you be sure to tell him how much he meant to me and how I wanted to give him everything in the world? I worry about that, Robert E. because I've seen and heard too much about that sort of thing happening. It's not about 'the other guys' all the time. Those stories you hear about on the news at night? That stuff's really happening here.

Same Day (Only Later)

Think about this Robert E. American colonist didn't like it when the British tried keeping house with them back in the 1700's. I believe that fueled this little thing called the American Revolution? We were a new country trying to escape the tyranny of another country located how many thousands of miles away across what ocean? Sound familiar? Now here we are, the United States in a country whose civilization dates thousands of years before our own and we think we're going to change anything? I think it'd be a different story if Iraq wasn't sitting on such a load of oil, don't you?

Let's Americanize the entire world! Sure, some countries could use a little tweaking here and there, but as far as trying to blatantly change an entire culture overnight and not expect any repercussion? It seems we've proved that we truly are an egotistical bunch. We decided to promote our idea of Democracy on uninterested/unwilling people. We chose this battle and wonder why these people don't embrace us and our culture? These days it's becoming harder and harder to determine who is glad we Americans are still here and who wishes we'd get out and leave them alone.

We're the self-appointed peace keepers of the entire world insisting on the necessity of occupying a country, an ancient civilization. (That's right. This isn't a war. It's only an occupation, Robert E.) In tracking the war on terrorism, we thought we'd try 'gently' encouraging/imposing American Democracy. This country has had its own conflict for thousands of years! They didn't need our help. How could we have expected to change anything, period? Let's encourage, let's allow Iraqis to vote and along the way let's stamp out terrorism! So long as it's the American way then all tactics are acceptable. Right now, I know a couple thousand Iraqis who would tell you different.

It's not been without good intention, but I've yet to see the 'gentle encouragement'. There was definitely no easing in and so far, no plans on how to help this country after we back out. We're Americans though, by God, and you're going to do things our way. We know what's good for the Iraqi citizens even if the Iraqi citizens don't know yet. We'll worry about consequences later.

20 August

You know how we've shut down all the bases stateside? They're talking about building permanent ones here, where the people don't want us. Why? What if China or Russia stomped into Texas or New York next week and tried doing the same thing we've done here? We've bombed this place all to pieces and now have to rebuild it. And how are we doing that? With big contractors from the States? Why can't we let all the unemployed Iraqis rebuild their own country? God knows there's enough of them; unemployed I mean. What are we waiting for? Give them their own sense of purpose? "Because we're the United States, not Burger King and you're not going to have it your way."

We've focused our concerns on Iraq but now the question is, has anybody stopped to wonder who may be plotting what next? Do we still even have task forces or committees analyzing data, chatter, whatever it is that they study at tax-payer's expense, to try figuring out what the next 9-1-1 is going to be? I think about that every time I turn out the light. I guess this letter makes me sound like a bad American, a bad Marine in the very least. I'm just ready to come home and live my life without having sand blown in my face; literally as well as figuratively. I'm tired of having a target on my head just because I'm an American. Honestly, I'm tired of being over here, period. Peace-keeper, defender of freedom or not, I'm ready to come home.

Well, duty calls. I must go meet the next group. I miss you and LB with all my heart. I don't know what else to write so I'll just ask of you this; tell my little one Mommy's coming home soon. I'm counting the days Robert E. The press doesn't wait…news at eight!

CHAPTER 16

THOUGHTS BEFORE

"Em, what exactly did you want to accomplish, as a Marine I mean?"

As much as she'd always talked about getting away, getting out of Arkansas, Emily started feeling like she'd been gone too long. With tired eyes, Emily anxiously started counting down the days until she would be home for good. Emily started seeing the situation in Iraq as unnecessary. Robert E. thought it ironic that within a week of his receiving what was to be her final letter, she finally did come home, was finally finished with having to think about the world or where she stood in it.

He remembered how she answered the question.

"What exactly did I want to accomplish? I wanted to become one of the few and the proud. I wanted to know I made a difference, that I wasn't just some inconsequential blip on somebody's radar. I did that, Robert E. I'm now a part of history, a part of a people's history and not just American history either. Most importantly, I did it out of tradition. None of my brothers were officers, you know. I did it for my dad. You know, never forget?"

"Be careful what we wish for, huh?" He asked the empty room.

Robert E. remembered Old Man Nichols. He was quite the character. Many times, especially with the older generations, a person could look at a man and automatically figure he must be a veteran. Emily's father was no exception. As easy-going and quiet-natured as he was, you just knew there was a proud, proud Marine behind that set of piercing, silver eyes. The Old Devil Dog had kept his uniform, too. "Don't believe I'll ever fit into it again-" He'd chuckled as he patted his belly, "- but I'll be damned if I don't have some grand memories of when I could." There were no emblems on the sleeves; no insignia across the shoulders save for his rank but the front held a colorful collection of ribbons and badges, a collection Mr. Nichols had obviously still been very proud of.

"I can still shoot, too by God." He'd thunder. "I could go outside right now and shoot the pins off the clothes line if I were so inclined." His eyes lit up as his thoughts traveled thousands of miles away, remembering battles fought beside his brothers. "They've written books about us, you know," The old man smiled and nodded his head. "-books, and song boy and ain't a one of 'em that tell the whole story."

Robert E. remembered there always being two flags flying at the top of the Nichols' driveway; Old Glory was proudly displayed atop of the first pole and right next to it stood the flag that flashed red in the wind that signified Marine. There certainly was an order about everything Old Man Nichols did, though he was never over the top. His very presence commanded respect, and he got it, too. Robert E. loved listening to him tell his stories. Even when some of those stories came round a second or third time, nobody ever confessed to hearing them before. Mr. Nichols was every bit a Marine all the way to the day he died.

Robert E. heaved a long, slow, sigh. "Well, someday sure came and went, didn't it?" He muttered to himself. "You never had to validate anything Em. Not with me." Emily's view of the war was more than from the eyes of small-town (sometimes small-minded) Arkansas. She understood the risks before she ever signed on the dotted line but that didn't mean she never tired of having to continuously close gates after the horses got out.

He reflected thoughtfully. "How many ladies wear hats to church anymore?" Robert E. asked the empty room. No matter how he tried to organize them, thoughts continued running through his mind in random, chaotic sequences. It wasn't anything new and Robert E. actually welcomed it that morning. Looking at his watch, he figured his folks and LB would be pulling in the driveway any minute. They'd play the game one more time; Mama telling him how they missed him at church, his father telling him how Rev Max had asked

about him. Robert E. wasn't making church a priority these days. Besides, he didn't feel like being micro-scrutinized by folks in the gallery.

"I'll just blame it on you again Emily." He smiled to himself.

CHAPTER 17

LOOKING BACK

It was another new chapter, or possibly the first one re-visited. Whatever it was, Robert E. wasn't sure what to call it. Repositioning himself on the floor, he reluctantly picked up the small, red velvet bag. Refocusing on the task before him, he poured its contents into his hands. He disregarded everything but the shiny pieces of metal that fell from within. He held her dog-tags in his hands, squeezing them tightly. Before Emily had gone back, she'd given Robert E. her extra set to hold onto, the ones he still wore around his neck. The set he held in his hand were those they brought to him before the funeral. He traced his finger across the letters and closed his eyes again, remembering.

"I'm counting the days, Robert E."

The last time Emily had come home on leave, he'd noticed something different about her. She was changed. He couldn't put a finger on any one thing, so subtle were the differences, but he could tell. There were noticeable peculiarities such as how she never sat with her back to a door and how she always made sure the lights didn't throw her shadow on a curtain. God forbid there were any unexpected or loud noises. The simple backfire from a car could make her jump a foot in the air. He'd witnessed that on more than one occasion. Robert E. never remembered her being that anxious or one who startled so easily.

Emily'd always been a quiet and reflective person but after she came home from Iraq the first time, she seemed even more quiet and reserved. With whatever the task at hand happened to be, she would come in, get it done, and get out; just like that. She didn't offer any of her usual chit-chat or banter. Filling in the empty spots with unnecessary conversation became a rare event.

He'd always have the memories, but he needed more than memories to come home to, to hold onto at night. How was he supposed to keep moving forward at this point in the game? He'd wasted too many precious years before determining to find her again and just when they had things going right, she'd gone back for one more hitch. He clutched the rounded, metal squares in his hand tightly and took a deep breath, exhaling slowly.

The unexplained premonitions and glimpses of déjà vu came to an abrupt halt the morning he came back to the house to soldiers greeting him in uniform. These days, more often than not, his mind was in a permanent fog. He continued trying to preoccupy himself with thoughts of her because those thoughts and memories were always the clearest. It wasn't anything he could explain. Occasionally some well-meaning person would offer supposition that he was experiencing depression but Robert E. shrugged off that explanation for two reasons. The first was simply the fact that he was a man and men like him didn't get depressed. He was as blue-collar as they got. Psychiatry was for wimps. The second entailed the fact that yes, he was having trouble letting go and moving forward but he, well, he just knew he wasn't depressed. End of discussion. He'd lost the love of his life. Was he not allowed to think of her or miss her?

He opened the small, leather-bound journal that had fallen from its nest among the bundles of letters and began writing.

Dear Emily:

You always asked me to stop and think about possibilities, about 'what ifs?' Like what if we had never reconnected? What if I hadn't been driving to work the morning you rolled your truck? What if you hadn't re-enlisted? We never talked about what if you never came home. I wouldn't let you. I always told you we never had to worry about that.

I know sometimes I wasn't a lot of things, but I never saw that in your eyes. When we reconnected, I realized how much you had to have held on by sheer hope for all these years, Emily. Hope was what got you through, got me back to you. I don't even have that to hold onto now.

I wasn't always the person you needed me to be. Sometimes I didn't pay enough attention or just flat out failed to see whatever point you were trying to make at the time. Who I always was though, was the type of guy who liked letting a person know I'd been reached. Emily, you reached me; every time. It took until you were gone for me to figure it out but you truly reached me.

Sometimes there's no point in truth-telling, especially if the only thing it's going to do is cause pain. But Em, I know better than that. The thing I worried about each time we got together was admitting to knowing any better. As far as I was concerned, I didn't. But I did. I always knew you wanted more. If only I had listened.

I know there were times when I was a son-of-a-gun, a real smart-alec. I mean, what was it you called me? Reprehensible;

a reprehensible jock. I'll never forget the day you said that. I didn't know what that word meant, (and I reckon I still don't) but I'll never forget it. Even after school was all said and done, you never let who I appeared to be affect the way you felt. If you did, you were too much of a lady to say anything. I suppose deep inside I knew exactly what I was doing, but never imagined how it would end, how we would end. I think you did. All those years and you still believed. You still believed there was an 'us' to consider. I don't know what kept you looking.

I'm scared of moving on and never feeling the rest of my life the way I felt when I was with you. I regret having wasted all the years, never seeing what was in front of me all along. The one thing we always were was the ones who were able to pick up where we left off and somehow I know that's what you had pictured for us now. Wherever you are, I figure you'll still be waiting for me. "Always late, Robert E. That's why I've left early." Only this time, I wish you hadn't left before. To cop a phrase from that movie, "when they ask me what I liked best, I'll still say it was you." Movie or not, that's how I feel.

Being alone has made me see a few things more clearly. It's been more closure I guess, but I finally get it. I figure I was supposed to make my mark on this world in ways other than those requiring my getting stuffed into the back of some police car or calling Dad for bail. I figured you were always going to be part of it all. Then all of a sudden you were gone. Somehow though, you left me reminders, you gave me memories. I was still seeing the world through your eyes. I don't know why else I'd still be finding you in all the things I do. I hope you will forgive me for acting like such a fool and consider the undertaking this was for me to admit, to write, and wish I could send. I miss you Em, more than you'll ever know.

Robert E. closed his eyes and took a deep breath, clenching his fist tightly around the set of dog-tags in his hand.

He'd just finished the impromptu entry in the journal when he heard the car roll down the driveway. He didn't notice that he'd dropped the little pieces of metal on the floor as he hurriedly scooped up the journal and all the pictures he had spread out earlier. Hastily shoving the red box under the bench behind him, he quickly picked the old coffee cup back up just as they walked through the door. LB didn't need to see all that spread across the floor.

"Neither do the folks for that matter." Robert E. spoke out loud. They knew quite well their son was still mourning Emily's loss.

"Missed you, Daddy." LB kicked off his shoes and ran straight for Robert E. who was still sitting on the floor drinking his cold coffee nonchalantly."Rev Max asked Grandma and Grandpa how you were." The little boy innocently revealed part of a conversation he probably had not been meant to overhear. "He always asks how you are."

"Your mother brought a church bulletin home for you." Jon Elliott bent over and picked up the silver beaded chain from the floor. "You forgot these, son." He studied Robert E.'s face carefully as he gently dropped the shiny pieces of metal into his son's hands.

"I'm sure she did." Robert E. took the chain and set it on top of the box he'd hastily shoved under the bench. "Rev still ain't givin' up, is he?" He pulled LB close in a bear hug, tickling his belly. "How 'bout a rib sandwich?" he asked the little boy.

"Daddy. Stop! Stop! I got to pee." LB squealed as he squirmed to get away. Robert E. immediately let him go and steered his son toward the bathroom.

"Okay, okay. You know where to go. Go on, get!" The little boy dutifully ran down the hall. "Don't forget to wash your hands."

"Bobby?"

Robert E. winced. Only Mama got away with calling him Bobby these days.

"Ma'am?"

"We missed you today. I brought you a bulletin" She looked around the living room. "What kept you, sweetheart?"

"I heard." Robert E. stood up respectfully, graciously accepting the little church note she offered, ignoring the last question completely. He glanced guiltily at his father. "Got up late."

"Service was nice today. Max always gives nice sermons. I'm sure you would've enjoyed it. He's always asking how you're doing." She glanced at her husband quickly but not before Robert E. noticed. "Where'd that young one get off to?" She could sense something unspoken between the two men and busied herself with looking after LB. "He's still in his church clothes."

"I'm sure I would have, Mama. You let me read this and I'll take some church later this evening." Robert E. held up the paper for her to see. It had become a ritual. Every Sunday, he awoke with no intentions of going to church and every Sunday she came home and told him how much everybody had missed him and "Here, I brought you a bulletin."

His mother acknowledged him with a tired, sad smile as she went to tend to LB. Despite the fact that he hardly ever made it to church anymore, she knew her son did read the weekly church bulletins she brought home. They'd raised a good set of children over the years and Bobby was no exception. Having him and LB at the house was almost like old times; almost. If it had not been for the circumstances that the two of them came to live back home, she could almost picture Emily still being there.

"Almost." Her thoughts turned briefly to her daughter-in-law. It seemed such a long time since they'd received the news. Bobby was so intent on making sure LB would never forget his Mama that he seemed to have forgotten about taking care of himself, always sifting through some box or another of photographs and papers, holding on to things for his sons' sake. In her opinion, Robert E. wasn't dealing with life after Emily well but she didn't know what to say to her son. The last thing she wanted to do was alienate him. Bobby never made it to church these days and she suspected the box she'd spied under the bench in the living room again had something to do with it today. She hadn't missed the glance exchanged between her husband and son as she walked through the door. Her mind raced back to that morning, picturing that moment in the kitchen as clearly as if it had happened yesterday. Not for the first time in her life, she had been witness to an unwelcome, yet necessary day.

CHAPTER 18

UNEXPECTED

LB and Robert E. had been staying at his parents' home for the weekend, something customary ever since Emily had deployed the last time. Anna had just finished putting breakfast dishes away and was getting ready to start preparing lunch when she noticed an unfamiliar vehicle prowling slowly down their road, cautiously pulling into their drive.

"Jon? Are there any dishes left in there?" She nervously picked up a dish towel. Her eyes riveted to the window as she continued watching. Anna hoped it was only somebody lost or looking for a place to turn around, but she knew it wasn't. She had watched and read enough about what was going on in Iraq to know what the vehicle probably meant.

The two men stepped out of the car, automatically falling into step with one another as they made their way to the door. Navy Lieutenant Commander William Gregory and Marine Colonel Donald Bradford were preparing themselves, thinking about the news they were about to deliver.

Don Bradford was thinking to himself, quietly reviewing the script in his mind. At this very moment, he and his team were the only people in the United States who knew this

Marine had been killed. Showing up at stranger's doors at virtually any hour in dress uniform unannounced, notifying the next of kin when a soldier died wasn't something anyone had to second-guess, was something nobody could sugarcoat. Though it was almost an obligatory responsibility, more than once his job had been called a disagreeable duty. After all, the military had developed thorough procedures and protocol to follow, approved scripts, just for such occasions. He'd been asked countless times over the course of years why he kept doing it. His answer came almost too readily.

"Semper Fidelis. Always faithful. No matter the occasion."

It wasn't as if this was the first time he'd had to complete such duty, not even the first time in this particular town. Bradford was already familiar with the streets here as he had completed a previous visit, performing the same sensitive task after another Marine in this town had been killed in Iraq. Today was no different. It was his sense of duty, his obligation, albeit a solemn one but one he took especially to heart; different day, different circumstances perhaps, but with no different consequence. Inevitably, as he walked to each door, he thought of all the Marines he'd known who'd gone to fight for their country, the ones who came home. Then he thought of all the ones who went to fight but never came back. With his job, he was helping bring another one of them home. It never got easier, stepping up to those unsuspecting doors and delivering the words a family would forever remember.

Bradford never knew what to expect with any of these calls. His little casualty notification team had searched for plenty of addresses, knocked on plenty of doors and introduced themselves to plenty of military spouses during the course of their work. Always prepared for the worst, they were the ones who put into words the inevitable, the words that family members always seemed to know before they ever answered the door.

It was generally implied that 'spouse' meant wife. Never yet had the person Bradford had to notify been a soldier's husband. That was about to change. The Marine's family he was about to inform today was a woman; Wilhelmina Emily Nichols Elliott. Unfortunately, there was a first time for everything.

"Papa? Where'd Bob and LB say they were going?" With forced calm, Anna called into the living room over her shoulder as she quickly dried her hands on the dish towel at the counter. Though he was a grown man, married, and had a child of his own, she'd always think of Bobby as one of her boys. Her eyes rimmed with tears she would not allow to fall.

"They went to the tracks to watch trains. Don't fret, Mama. Bob said they'd be back in plenty of time for lunch." The elder Mr. Elliott noisily folded the paper he held in his hands and was about to walk out into the kitchen. "Let me help you finish up out there. Sounds like we got company this morning."

Straightening his tie and giving his uniform a self-conscious brush with his hand, Bradford looked at the chaplain. "Here we go."

Three sharp knocks resounded through the Elliott house.

Anna drew in a slow, deep breath. Though over forty years had passed, she knew what that car and the uniforms in it represented. It wasn't something she'd ever forget. Back then, there wasn't a car full of soldiers giving the news, but her mother knew.

Anna walked into the dining room just in time to see Jon open the door. Standing before him were two men, their solemn composure accentuated by the uniforms they wore. Officers;

one Colonel, one Lieutenant. Anna knew her military ranks. Notice wasn't given by cold telegrams any more.

"I'm Colonel Donald Bradford, Casualty Assistance Officer and this is Lieutenant William Gregory."

Gregory nodded in quiet acknowledgment.

"We are here to speak with Robert Anthony Elliot, Sr. May we step inside?"

"Yes, yes of course." Jon Elliot stepped back to allow the two men into the living room. His eyes briefly met Anna's as the men filed in and immediately removed their hats.

"I'm Jon, Jon Elliot, Bobby's-I mean, Robert's father. Is this about Emily? Something's happened to her. Has she been hurt? Is she alright?"

Anna interrupted, "Won't you sit down-" praying she was wrong. But she knew.

Don Bradford remained silent, waiting until Jon Elliott had closed the door before speaking again. Purposefully placing his hat under his left arm, he turned to Jon Elliott. "Sir, I need to speak directly to Mr. Elliott." Per protocol, he refrained from disclosing further detail.

"Of course." Jon Elliot said again as he looked first to the door than at Anna.

Bradford was an undeniably experienced officer with exceptional leadership skills. As an accomplished career Marine, he had attained a proven combat record defined by a wall of framed commendations earned throughout his years spent as an officer in the Corps. He was a Marine, serving his country proudly. Besides combat and leadership, Don Bradford was also experienced in something else, something he was equally proud of. He was a casualty affairs officer. It wasn't a pleasant duty, was sometimes dangerous, but unfortunately necessary. His job was something that had to be done.

Casualty affairs. The job never entailed simply knocking on a door, delivering the news and walking away. Every door was different, no reaction ever the same. No matter what the response, Bradford had to be prepared. There was only so much information he was able to give with the initial call, often a make or break situation with the family or spouse at the receiving end. Families never forgot how they received the news or how the situation was handled.

"Of course," Jon repeated. "We're expecting the boys home any moment. You might as well sit down." The elder Mr. Elliot fought to hold his emotions in check. It was obvious the officers before him had their own feelings concerning the task at hand as they politely acknowledged the offer but remained standing.

Bradford looked puzzled at the reference Jon Elliot had made. "Boys?"

"His son." Jon answered absently as he went to stand vigil at the big bay window in the living room. Feeling almost obligated, he added, "Six years old." He continued watching out the window, avoiding anyone's eyes, watching up the road. Jon Elliott knew his son would see the strange vehicle in the drive. He'd already know. Bobby wouldn't have to be told.

Just as John Elliott had predicted, it was only minutes before Robert E. and LB came running down the road, playfully chasing one another like sons and fathers do as they made their way down the driveway. Jon Elliott watched as his son paused by the government vehicle, shooing LB onto the porch.

Robert E's chest tightened as he first looked at the car and then at the house, his eyes meeting his father's gaze at the window. The elder Mr. Elliott didn't move. There was immediate understanding in Robert E.'s eyes and he quickly followed behind LB. For Robert Anthony Elliott that was the moment Iraq went from being the formerly obscure country thousands of miles away to being the place in the middle of a desert where his wife died.

"Grandma, we're hungry like bears!" LB burst into the house, still excited from watching trains with his daddy. He hadn't taken notice of the strange vehicle in the driveway that still had its motor running. The little boy stopped short as he noticed the men in uniform.

"Daddy, look." LB pointed at the visitors. Though he was only three-years-old at the time, LB knew the men in the kitchen were important people. "Did you bring my mom home?" He asked innocently, still in a playful mood from playing tag with his father.

"Anna, maybe you should take LB upstairs." Jon Elliott suggested softly as he watched the blood drain from his youngest sons' face.

"No Mama, leave him stay. Come here LB." The little boy obediently ran to his fathers' side. Robert E. picked him up, hugging his son tightly against his chest.

Both men waited for the moment. Bradford turned to Robert E.

Judging from the expression of dread on the man's face, Bradford already knew this was Robert Elliott.

"Robert Elliott?" Robert E. nodded numbly.

"I'm Major Donald Bradford and this is Lieutenant Commander William Gregory."

Robert E. waited quietly, without expression, bracing himself for the news he already knew. He was officially about to be told he was a widower.

"On behalf of the United States Marines-"

In an inordinately composed response, Robert E. held up a hand softly interrupting the officers' noticeably scripted presentation. "Save it. I already know. How'd it happen?"

Bradford took a deep breath. Looking Robert E. straight in the eye, he launched into the notification he had prepared. "The commandant of the United States Marine Corp has entrusted me to express with deep regret that your wife, Major Wilhelmina Nichols Elliott was killed in the Al Ambar Province of Fallujah, Iraq when a suicide bomber intercepted the vehicle she was in while guiding a press group-"

Anna involuntarily gasped.

"Who got lost Daddy?" LB asked naively, interrupting Bradford. "Is my mom home?"

Bradford looked at Robert E. who raised his hand again, shook his head and closed his eyes. "I'll handle it." Robert E. didn't hear anything else after he was told Emily had been killed. He immediately felt as if he'd been punched in the gut, the wind knocked out of him. People weren't supposed to get killed for anything less than duty to their country. Suicide-bomber? That only made it that much harder to accept. All he could think of was the conversation he and Emily had about the women with Down's syndrome and the exploding donkeys. He laughed in spite of himself, not at the misfortune of the woman or even the donkeys but just the irony of it all.

"When?"

Robert E. finally asked out loud, visibly straining to hold his emotions in check. He enunciated the word with tremendous difficulty, trying to think of something more but the words wouldn't come.

Bradford didn't have to look down once to the papers he held in his hand for answers to any of the questions Robert E. asked. Too many times, the officer experienced the quick memorization of facts; answers to questions that families almost inevitably asked. This time was different though. Robert Elliott asked very few questions. When Bradford responded, he glanced first at Jon Elliott who in turn studied his son's face.

When Robert E. spoke again, it was in a voice Jon had never heard before (or since.) "Let me get this straight. We've bombed Iraq. We've got Hussein. We showed all the people over there what America does best. I'd like to know what we're still doing there."

Don Bradford didn't respond, continuing to listen impassively.

"It's the same story all over again. Does anyone else not see it?" Robert E. blurted out. "Same place, essentially same reason, just a different person." He trailed off, knowing they expected him to be emotional. How was a person supposed to act or speak after hearing something like that? Instead, he blurted out the first thing that came to mind. "What was she doing at the front in the first place? I thought women weren't allowed in combat. She was a woman, for Christ's sake. I mean public affairs of all things."

Bradford shifted his balance before responding. It was a delicate situation, knowing what to say, how much to tell the families about how their family member died.

"Guiding press was only one of her duties." Too much information could be just as bad as too little. At initial notification, only the most critical information was made available. Despite all the questions family members inevitably asked, the team could only answer so much. It'd been in Bradford's experience to expect the unexpected when it came to notifying next of kin. Grief affected people in singular ways and he couldn't tell which way this was going.

Going against the scripted guidelines he was supposed to follow, Bradford spoke more about Emily. "Mr. Elliott, you are correct. Your wife wasn't in a combat position." The officer paused. Nobody spoke. "However, it's difficult to define where the front actually is from one day to the next." To himself, the officer thought, "Hey, no kidding. Nobody's safe from bombs or rockets."

Oblivious to Bradford's voice, Robert E. remembered clearly the conversation he and Emily'd had about a high ranking female officer who was killed around Christmas several years back. She'd brought it up several times during the course of their regular conversations.

"What made you think of that?" Robert E. stopped what he was doing as he waited for her to continue.

"She was doing the same job I have." Emily whispered. She took a moment to compose herself and continued, speaking soft and low. "Robert E. I listened to the guns today, I mean, I really listened. You know, some guys here can tell you how far away gunfire is just by listening. So I tried it. I listened, I mean really listened hard and you know, all I heard was pop-pop-thunk. A medic told me the 'thunk' was probably somebody getting shot. He was serious, almost scary serious. He said he knew by the sound, Robert E. What if-"

"Hey, let's not think about 'what if'. It's war. Sometimes, something has to give." He wasn't sure how to respond to the silence at the other end of the line. When Emily still had not said anything, he understood her seriousness. "You're not gonna be a 'what if', Emily." Robert E. said quietly, trying to reassure her. Of course he thought about 'what if?' All the time. He thought about it every single day, every single time he spoke to her. It was always a possibility. What if?

"Escorting press, just like that other gal." Robert E. thought out loud.

The officer nodded his head slowly. "Your wife was in-"

"You don't have to tell me where she was. I know." Robert E. interjected bitterly. "I know she wasn't home." Robert E. responded, his voice rising. He was in a state of disbelief. "Emily wasn't just another body doing a job. She was a wife; a mother. She wasn't supposed to die in some foreign country." For Robert E., that was the day the war in Iraq ended.

"Mr. Elliott, a casualty assistance officer will be contacting you to discuss your preferences for-"

Jon Elliott cleared his throat and shook his head at Bradford.

His job was done but the task was far from complete. Bradford knew it was just the beginning for this family. Looking at Robert E. but speaking to Jon, he briefly informed them of when Robert E. could expect Emily's personal belongings. Robert E. remained silent allowing his father to speak for him.

Before they left, Don Bradford handed a business card to Jon Elliott.

"If you should have any questions…"

To this day, memories from that morning were still a blur to Robert E. There'd been so much to process, so many questions he wanted to ask but hadn't been able to find the words for. Everything about that morning had been unexpected. He never figured he'd be receiving news like that period, much less at the breakfast table on a Monday morning, on any morning. Emily was dead. Not gone, not passed away. Dead. They told him she died escorting a press group? A press group? What were press groups doing in combat zones? Jon Elliott had remained at his son's side asking questions as Robert E. sat impassively, only nodding in disbelief.

There were always going to be endings to face, especially with regard to war. It was rare to have truly happy ones and in Don Bradford's experience, there were almost never any 'happily ever afters.' Robert E. had contemplated details from that horrible morning more than once over the past few years.

The cedar box Emily had entrusted to him became a destiny, a time-machine of sorts. Anything reminding him of her, he automatically placed in that box, always intending to 'sort through it eventually'. It was later that evening when he'd replaced her dog tags with the letter the sergeant major had read to him that Robert E. finally gave in and let himself break down. Alone. Privately. He clearly remembered the details from that morning, the day his world fell apart.

Robert E. had been thankful that night when his mother took LB upstairs for the evening. He and LB were supposed to return to their own home that morning but ended up staying with his folks for a few more days after finding themselves the recipients of that catastrophic news. The little boy had scooted off to bed without any argument knowing that something serious, something bad had happened but not grasping the exact caliber of the news that had been relayed. Robert E. knew he'd have to sit down with LB to tell him what happened to Emily but he needed time himself to process the information before he felt up to that task. His boy was barely three years old, both a blessing and a curse. LB wouldn't remember that day but neither would he remember his mother.

CHAPTER 19

LOST BUT STILL LOOKING

Memories; not always good things. Robert E. tried hard to get back to sleep but his brain wasn't cooperating. His mind was constantly spinning between the present and the past; here one minute, a thousand miles away the next, fast-forward, sudden rewind, never pausing in between.

For countless nights after he'd received the news, sleep eluded Robert E. For him, time had stopped; trapping him in the events from that morning years ago. Aspects of that day played constantly in his mind, relentlessly repeating; over and over again. "We regret to inform you…" "Emily died…" This particular night was no different. It finally came to the point that Robert E. finally felt obliged to get up and turn on the lights only to lay back down on the middle of the bed and continue staring at the ceiling. Folding his hands behind his head, he let out a long sigh and looked around the room. His eyes fell on the church bulletin on the nightstand.

"Said I'd read it." He said to the empty room, glancing at the glowing numbers on the clock that he'd been watching change throughout the night. "Guess four in the morning is as good a time to take my church as any." It wasn't exactly what

148

he wanted to be doing at that hour of the morning but he had promised. As he reached over and picked up the glossy 5X7 church bulletin, Robert E. heard a soft knock at the door.

"Bobby?" His father's sleepy voice asked softly. "You okay, boy?"

Robert E. smiled a slow, drowsy, melancholy smile. "Yes sir."

"Can I come in?"

"Sure."

His father opened the door, nodding with silent approval as he saw the bulletin in his sons' hands.

"Couldn't sleep." Robert E. waved the papers at his father who remained standing in the doorway. "Figured I'd make good to Mama."

"You haven't been asleep any night this hour these past few weeks." The old man stifled a yawn. "You're gonna take sick if you don't watch yourself."

"How would you know I've not been sleepin' unless you ain't been neither? Why you been up so?" Robert E. looked at the increasingly noticeable lines etched at the corners of his father's eyes. "What's your story?"

"Aw, don't have a story, boy. It's plain fact. Just wait, you'll be in the same boat if you live long enough. The gals ain't the only ones who got things changin' as they get older." His father grinned. "It ain't by choice you hear me walking down the hall in the middle of the night. Yer Ma, now she'll sleep through just about anything but let LB sneeze cross-ways and she's up like a shot." He nodded self-assuredly. "She was like that with every one of you kids, too.

Bobby, yer Mama knows you ain't been restin' easy. Can't hide stuff like that from a mama. She's worried about you, son and quite frankly, so am I."

"I know, Daddy. I appreciate that. It's just this time of year, I-" Robert E. trailed off. "You know how it goes. Seems 'round this time every year, all I see are reminders. It doesn't even have to be pictures. Like one night awhile back, I found a letter she'd written. Don't know when she wrote it, either. I mean, LB and I were getting ready for the move and there it was. Bam! Sometimes I'll be thinking of her and one of her favorite songs starts playing on the radio. You know, everything used to be so clear," Robert E. paused. "-but I see everything all gray now. Actually, not even that. Things are dark. Still. I've prayed for help, but lately it's been real, real quiet as far as gettin' any answers. You know? All I see is her." Robert E. took a slow, deep breath. "I know, I shouldn't be angry with God, but I am."

"Coincidence, boy. A person generally sees whatever they want to see when they look at something long enough." The elder Mr. Elliott waited for his son's response.

"No such thing, Daddy. It's been like this ever since we were in school. I can't explain it. She and I, well we didn't even have to be together and it was like we knew what each other was thinking. I'd have thoughts just come to mind from out of nowhere and the phone would ring or I'd feel like I just had to call her at that absolute moment and we'd get talking and find out we were thinking about the same thing. Coincidence? No, I don't think so." Robert E. doubled up the pillow behind his head. "I mean, what's that all about? How can I just quit thinking about her? Was I supposed to be able to flip some switch?"

"Nobody's telling you to leave her go son,"His father fell silent. "-but you do still have to live." The elder Mr. Elliott studied his son's face a moment, choosing his next words carefully. "If it truly was just during this time of year, I wouldn't be worrying so much, son. The problem is, it's been every day since the morning you got the news. It'll be four years here pretty soon Bob..." He trailed off as Robert E. closed his eyes in frustration.

"I know." Robert E. glanced at the bulletin in his hands then looked at her picture on the dresser across the room. "It doesn't feel like she should be gone. It's like she's still stationed in Iraq. I miss her, Dad."

His father responded quietly as his gaze followed Robert E.'s. "We all do, boy. I'm not tellin' you I know how you feel but I suspect it's about time you moved ahead at least a little bit, maybe go see somebody. Maybe start out by talking to Max, I don't know."

Robert E. nodded in acknowledgment. Max the family preacher had known him his entire life. But it was Max. Robert E. wasn't comfortable with talking about how he felt to anyone, much less the preacher who had run the church as far back as he could remember.

"Bobby," Jon Elliott paused as he searched for just the right words, "-somehow you've got to get on with the business of livin'. Right now, you got too tight a hold on the past, boy. You ain't leavin' any room for the present. Though it doesn't much matter how I feel about it, does it? It's your life and you've got to live it like you see fit but remember; it ain't all about you.

You got that boy to consider, too. You have to start pullin' yourself together, son. Start livin' instead of barely existin'."

"Believe me. I know." Robert E. knew his parents both wanted him to go see somebody about how he was feeling but he just couldn't bring himself to do it. He'd fight his own battles on his own terms without help from anyone.

The older Elliott nodded. Sometimes he didn't know what to say to his son. It was hard watching him miss that girl. Emily was like another daughter to him and it'd hurt him too, when she was taken from their lives so unexpectedly.

"You know, we lost one of your Mama's brothers back in the day."

"Yeah. Uncle Lou, right? I was just thinking about that." Robert E. interrupted as Jon nodded his head. "I don't remember much about him. Was he and Mama close?"

"Ah Bobby. I ain't no good at remembering things like that." The elder Elliott looked thoughtful as he remembered that day years ago. "Been a long time. He was a good kid though. Your grandmother wasn't too thrilled with sending sons off to war. That woman didn't care about Viet Nam in the slightest."

"I don't remember Mama talking a whole lot about him. Shoot, I don't remember her talking a whole lot about her family period. See, I don't want LB to forget Emily like that. I just don't know what to do. On the one hand, I know I need to pull myself together but on the other, I feel like I'm leaving her somewhere. You know everything we went through before we got married, Daddy. She believed in me, she came back, and she waited. For years." Robert E. closed his eyes and took in a slow, deep breath. "I feel like I owe her something but I don't know what to give." He opened his eyes and shook his head. "I just don't know."

"Bobby, she did the uniform proud, son. Woman or not. She was a Marine. They don't just give out those uniforms you know. Why else you think their motto is "the few, the proud?""

Jon sensed his son still wasn't ready to reveal his exact feelings. The elder Mr. Elliott slowly stood up. "Be sure you really read that. You know your Ma." He hated seeing his son like this but at the same time, understood Robert E.'s reluctance to ask for any help. He only hoped it wouldn't kill him first.

"Quiz at eight. I know."

The men smiled with comfortable acknowledgment.

"Some things never change." Robert E. knew his mother would follow up on the bulletin she brought home. She'd never been one to force her own thoughts about church or religion onto her children but she did expect them to respect her beliefs. So as not to spoil her children's own budding viewpoints, it was a careful balance she was sure to maintain.

"Glory to God for that. Well, I'm up for the day. See you at the breakfast table, son." Jon Elliott felt the same as his wife did about religion. His faith had been shaken though, unquestionably so. It didn't mean he'd lost faith.

"Dad, let me ask you something. Wouldn't you think that in this day and age it'd be acceptable for everyone to do their church business from their own type of pew?" Robert E. immediately recalled a conversation with Emily.

"Bob, if that were true, she'd have never gone back."

Robert E. sat in silent contemplation. "What do you mean, Dad? I was talking about church."

"I know what you were talkin' about. I'm just telling you something you need to hear. Emily returned to fulfill an obligation, boy. Nobody decides to be a Marine just because they look good in the uniform. A person decides to go that route because of the challenge, the sense of achievement. When the Marines tell you to jump, Son, you jump and ask if was high enough later. You do what you're told without question. Bobby, you weren't going to stop her. It was a matter for somebody else's hands. All we could do was pray. Or, depending on the way you believe, you went to your thinking place or talking place or whatever other place you had." Robert E. looked up sharply as his father made the comment. "The point is, she had a place, too. Her thing may have been all about chance and circumstance or just plain meant to be but when all was said and done and she did her talking or praying or looking to the sky... she did what she believed in. Oh, you know other people will have lots to say about what she did or why she did it, and you know folks generally do," Jon looked hard into his son's eyes "-she was a gal that accomplished more in half a lifetime than most people do their entire duration. Son, she was a Marine. How many other women do you know who've accomplished that much? Do you think nobody's speculated 'bout that? If Emily didn't believe in her own decisions, if nobody dared to doubt her or have their own opinions, do you think she would've gone back? That gal had some stones."

"She said she wanted to make a difference, Dad. She wanted to help change things in this world."

"Then you have to believe that she did. She believed in what she was doing. So should you." Jon Elliott studied his son's face carefully. "They call that legacy, don't they? Look son," Jon Elliott lowered his voice. "-even Marines have got to die. Semper Fi doesn't make anyone bulletproof but there's something about being a Marine that's supposed to make that easier to accept. She died serving her country. Doesn't that make you proud of what she did?"

"You'd better get back to bed before Mama wakes up. I'm okay. Don't stay up. It's too early. Go back to bed."

"Well all right then."

Never too old for talks with the old man. Robert E. listened as his father made his way down the hall, briefly pausing at LB's door before retiring to his own room. He heard the click of their door and his father speaking softly to his mother in reassuring tones.

"Just a little talk with Bobby. No Sweetheart. Everything's all right. LB's fine. Go back to sleep. Sweet dreams."

"'Night Mama. Night Daddy." Robert E. whispered and began reading.

Do you know your purpose today? Or is it just another day? Are you going through the motions of the same routine? If you're a child of God, know that he has assigned a purpose for you this day. Sometimes you may lose focus on that fact and forget whose purpose you are set on this earth to fulfill. Fulfilling your purpose doesn't mean everything will be completed as planned. Why? Interruptions. There are irritating and often unplanned interruptions that arrive at the most inconvenient times, forcing you to put your own much-thought out plan aside and instead give attention to something you'd rather not deal with. "In his

heart, a man plans his cause but the Lord determines his steps." Our tragedies are God's tools. What we do with them is determined by circumstance. It is the gifts given by God that help us in any situation. The gift of life is the most sacred of all.

CHAPTER 20

SLUMBER

He didn't remember what time it came about, but sleep finally embraced Robert E. It wasn't a deep, restful slumber he was hoping to pull off but it would have to do to get him through another day. He awoke close to nine the next morning only because LB was trying unsuccessfully to slip quietly through the door.

"Sorry Daddy. Grandma told me not to bother you. Don't tell, okay?"

Robert E. sat up sleepily and looked at his little boy. "Aw, you ain't bothering me, boy. I was already awake. Now get up here and give your daddy a big hug." He patted the side of the bed. Four solid hours of sleep was the most he had gotten in some time.

"LB? Where'd you go?" Grandma's voice rang down the hall. She knew exactly where the little boy was. It was a game she and LB played every morning.

"Grandma's coming Daddy! Hide me! Hide me, quick!"

"Scrunch up behind the pillows. Don't wiggle. I'll hide you." Robert E. laughed with his son. Grandma would know exactly where to look for LB. She always knew.

"LB! Where are you?" Mama opened the door, peeking her head inside. "Oh dear, Bobby, have you seen a little boy come running through here lately? I seem to have misplaced my grandson again." LB couldn't contain his excitement and jumped from his hiding place behind the mountain of pillows.

"Here I am Grandma! I didn't wake my dad. He was already up. Tell her Daddy."

"He's right. I was already getting up. Dad up?" Robert E. knew his father was up and out the door by five every morning, rain or shine, 365 days a year. It was another routine he humored his mother with.

Nodding her head, Anna replied, "You know him. He's already been up town and back. I've started breakfast so you two get dressed and meet us at the table."

By the time Robert E. and LB had dressed and made it downstairs, Jon Elliott was just coming in from feeding the animals and throwing half a cord of wood into the cellar. Though it wasn't as much of a working farm anymore, Jon Elliott had kept enough animals to keep himself busy on a daily basis. Every morning, there were always a few hogs to feed and eggs to collect.

"That beagle's gonna throw her pups any day now. She won't let me near her." Jon Elliott referenced one of his more profitable pastimes; breeding hunting dogs.

"Daddy, I could have stacked wood for you." Robert E. felt guilty about sleeping in on a Monday morning. Back in the day, sleeping past seven was a big no-no, even on weekends. As it were, Jon Elliott still awoke before the crack of dawn every day of the week.

"Nonsense. That's the reason we kept the wood stove. It wasn't only because Mama insisted, you know. Cuttin' wood keeps me young. Besides, if I wanted you to put any wood down, I'd have told you to put some down, right?"

"Grandpa, you get to sit by me." LB cheerfully called out into the living room. He was already seated near the end of the long dining room table, impatiently waiting for the stack of pancakes Anna was preparing for him at the stove. "Grandma, don't cut mine. I can do it. I'm a big boy, you know."

"Yes LB. I know that all too well. Your daddy should have put a brick on your head to keep you little." Anna smiled to herself as she continued cooking breakfast.

"By God, it's darn right cold out there this morning." Jon Elliott called into the dining room as he took off his quilted flannel jacket and hung it behind the door. He walked into the rustic kitchen, breathing in the familiar smells of breakfast.

"Jon Elliott!" Anna gently admonished her husband. "LB's sitting right there. Mind what you say at this table, please." She brandished her spatula toward the table.

"I wasn't at the table just yet, Mama." Jon grinned. "And I wasn't cursing. Darn isn't as bad as what I was thinking. I'll bet he's heard worse things than that, anyway." He winked at Robert E. and LB. "Right, boy?"

"Not in this house he hasn't." Anna said from the stove.

Jon put his hands up in mock defense. "Easy, Mama. Point taken. You got a hot shot of coffee for me over there by chance?"

Robert E. watched as his father took his seat at the head of the table next to LB, noticing how his father moved a little slower than he used to as he made his way from the door to the table. After all, despite the demeanor of a man more in his fifties or sixties, Robert E. was extremely conscious of the fact his parents were both fast approaching their eighties.

"Yes Papa. Sit. Breakfast is almost ready." Even though he was a grown man, Robert E. still couldn't help but chuckle when his parents called each other Mama and Papa. It was something they did whenever any children (grown as they all were) or grandchildren were around. They'd explained it to the family once during one of their annual gatherings.

"It's not that unusual, really. We did it so none of you kids would call us by our name. We got plenty of strange looks over the years for doing it, of course but none of you kids ever hollered out for Jon or Anna, always Mama and Papa just like God intended. We done it for so long it just sort of stuck."

Anna poured her husband a cup of coffee from the ancient, sage green percolator pot plugged in next to the stainless finished microwave. Robert E. took immediate notice of the cup she pulled out of the cupboard. It was a pearl-glazed mug from the set he mused over the previous morning.

"Mama, I've got a brand new Black and Decker pot still in the box that you can have. It's one of those you hang under your cabinet to save counter space. I'll put it up this morning after breakfast if you'd like. It won't take ten minutes."

"No sir. You'll do no such thing. Don't you like how I fix the coffee?" His mother teased as she continued making pancakes at the grill. "I know it's not Starbucks but-"

"Sure Mama, I just thought-" Robert E. started.

"No, son. You didn't think." Anna turned to the table with a sparkle in her eye. "I like this old coffee pot. It's never quit on me so I've never quit on it. I'm surprised it still works after all the years it's got on it, but I still like it never-the-less. Besides, you're gonna need that Black and Decker space-saving pot for yourself when you and LB get back into your own place."

Robert E. looked up sharply. "Sorry Mama. I just-"

"Oh heavens, I didn't mean-" Anna was instantly beside herself as she realized how Robert E. had taken the comment.

Jon tactfully interrupted. "I think what mother means is she likes things just the way they are and isn't in any hurry to change anything, including you boys staying here."

"That's precisely what I meant. Now Bobby, you and LB want fried eggs with your flapjacks or would you rather I scramble you some?"

"I want my eggs without no yolks on them, please Grandma." LB cheerfully responded.

"Okay LB. Eggs without any yolks, coming right up." She emphasized 'any', gently correcting her grandson. Anna looked at Robert E. as she repeated LB's request. No yolks. That was how Emily always asked for her eggs. Her son wasn't the only one missing Emily. Anna's heart went out to LB every time she looked at him. Except for looking at photos and by what he was told, the little boy would never know his mother.

"It's okay Mama. I'm just thinking too hard again. You know me. This time of year don't help any. I'm sorry." Doesn't, Anna thought, silently correcting her son. The holidays were one reason why Robert E. felt the need to come back and stay with his parents. It wasn't so much the fact they were getting on in years as it was for his mother's ability to cheer him up and keep him there. That and the fact his parents' home always had a festive mood about it this time of year. LB didn't need a constantly brooding father to remind him of the empty spot in their own home.

"You've nothing to be sorry about, Bobby. How many pancakes would you like? I have enough batter left for everyone to eat their fill so don't tell me you won't have any." Anna had automatically shifted back into her usual joyful mode and the atmosphere in the kitchen brightened immediately.

The late summer/early fall rush of contractor work had run its predictable course and winter was steadily threatening to creep in. Robert E. had put the house up for sale just in time for the recession that the government and nobody else wanted to acknowledge.

It wasn't as if he was hard up for money, but it was all he could do to continue his every day routines in a house that only echoed how empty it had become. Emily'd loved that little house, anxious to expand and build. She had talked about settling in one place, looking forward to saving and collecting the things for their home that would proclaim longevity, her intentions of forever. The memories already scattered all over the place were testament to that. He remembered her expression the day he'd told her the house was theirs. That house was a part of her. When it came time to pack the final boxes, Robert E. thought he'd feel some sense of relief, some sense of closure; but he didn't. In some respects, it was finally over, but in others, it would never end. In the grand scheme of things, he felt as if he were betraying her, leaving her behind which was the last thing he had intended.

"At least I have good things to remember." He had stood in the empty hall looking down the stairs to the open living space below. She was gone but the house wouldn't let go, not completely. Not for the last time, circumstances intervened.

At first, in the days immediately following Emily's death, Robert E. found himself continuously avoiding references to the war in Iraq. If anything showed up on television, he changed the channel. If the radio started touting anything military, he turned it off. If anybody asked about Emily, he was suddenly busy or had to be somewhere else. He knew how people were talking and he knew what they were saying. He just couldn't shut off the memories after a prescribed number of days or weeks. Robert E. couldn't figure out how long he was supposed to remember. Two months? Three years? What? What was the magic number?

"It's been over six months, Anna." Mrs. Greeley had commented to his mother quietly at the grocery store. "When my Thomas died, I finished all that grief business in six months." Though she may have meant well, Robert E. knew he wouldn't have kind words to respond to Mrs. Greeley's remark with so he made sure to detour down the magazine aisle. She didn't know he had only been the next aisle over and heard every word.

As he waited for his mother to round the corner, Robert E. took notice of the variety of magazines displayed at eye level. Impulse purchases, things people bought because of some headline that caught their eye. "Famous So and So Caught Cheating on Wife" "The Year's Most Explosive Hollywood Divorces." "Medical Examiner Releases Long Waited Report on Star's Death." The magazines weren't even stories about people anyone in Mena knew, yet shoppers grabbed them up as if their lives depended on it.

"I bet nobody fights for the Times when a soldier gets killed." Robert E. thought bitterly. As much as he tried to figure it out, he could never understand people's fascination with the tragedy of other people's lives. Apparently, so long as the bad stuff was happening to somebody else, reading about it didn't seem like such a bad thing.

On more than one occasion, Robert E. thought about how many ways there were to contend with the pain, with the void left in his life. He'd never been a big drinker and other than the occasional weekend football game, rarely drank at all. But ever since Emily was killed, he really wanted to drink, if only to make reality go away for a little while, make everything like it used to be. And that's how it generally worked, if he was lucky,. He respected his parents enough to never drink in the house. Besides, he didn't want his son to witness his inebriation. He'd leave LB with his parent's and go back to the empty house to have private, alcohol-induced conversations with Emily. He drank his beer, got drunk and in his mind, there was never a problem. After awhile though, the beer wasn't enough and he started relying on whiskey; hard. It wasn't the cheap brand either; top shelf.

"Only the best for you, Emily. If I'm going to do this, least I should do it right. Semper Fi." By Fate or circumstance, Robert E. never made it out the door, passing out to sleep it off one more time. His folks knew where he went. They knew what he was doing, but they couldn't stop him. Jon Elliott had driven by the little house on more than one occasion to confirm what he already suspected. He never knew how close his son came to ending his pain once and for all.

Robert E. tried a few spouse-support meetings but quickly realized that wasn't going to work. (The whiskey worked better.) He was a definite minority, sitting among those wives, not missing some of the contemptuous looks cast his way. A trip to the zoo for the kids, hanging out with children of fathers who were still in or killed over in Iraq was good for LB but Robert E. felt out of place. Every meeting, every event was the same thing; women complaining about their new, unexpected rolls as single-parents, primary caretakers, homemakers who suddenly had to man-up to financial responsibilities, the day-to-day chores ordinarily taken care of by their husbands that they never worried about suddenly thrust upon them. He never said a word. Robert E. didn't want to minimize those spouses who were struggling to exist and realized how fortunate he and Emily'd had it. Financially, they were already fine. There were bills to pay, groceries to buy, and a house to clean whether she was home or not. They'd always shared those duties even before she was deployed, and it was no different now. Just lonelier because he knew she was never coming home. Robert E. didn't have anything in common with any of those women so he quit going to the meetings. He couldn't understand how they perceived their problems to have been "unexpectedly dropped into their laps". They were military wives. They knew the possibilities when they married into the whole military scene. It was one thing to not want anything to happen, to change, but to never expect the possibility? September 11 was a vulgar wake-up call. How were they all caught so off-guard? It wasn't like it was the 1940's or 50's when women rarely worked outside the home or didn't know how to keep a checkbook.

"Did people enlist and think we were never going to have a war?" Robert E. kept his thoughts to himself. To him, it seemed everyone at those meetings had ignored the most basic Boy Scout motto; "Be prepared."

One night just before the house sold, Robert E. went back one more time to be alone. While sitting on the living room floor arguing with one of Emily's memories, Robert E. stopped mid-sentence. He looked around, looked at his hands. Here he was, sitting on the floor, alone in this big, empty house arguing with his dead wife. He wasn't anybody's husband anymore. He was a widower, a single parent. He looked at the half-empty bottle, knowing he had a choice to make. On one hand, he had nothing, not anymore. In the other, he held the bottle that was helping him through the depression he had finally acknowledged. The pain of losing her, the anguish of never holding her in his arms again was more bearable when he drank. Looking at that demon in his now trembling hand, he thought briefly about how easily he could tip the bottle back, finish it off and ease the truck into the garage; leave it running. Shut the door. Too easy. He looked back at his empty hand. It wasn't totally empty. Robert E. took a deep breath and released it slowly, instantly feeling ashamed. What was he thinking? He was too wrapped up in pitying himself that for a brief moment, he'd failed to recognize what he still had. LB. That little boy had already lost his mama.

"Coward." He cursed himself. That time, Robert E. somehow pulled himself up.

On the outside, he knew things had to get back to some semblance of normalcy, if only for LB's sake. But for Robert E., it was more than just having his wife taken from him; a part of his soul was taken as well. Slowly working his way through his grief, Robert E. started to understand that the things between he and Emily weren't governed strictly by circumstances and chance. All that stuff Emily had ever said about Fate slowly started to make sense.

CHAPTER 21

LONG ENOUGH

Letting go was a painfully slow process, almost tortuous. That was why Robert E. couldn't do it or at least was reluctant to do so. No matter what the circumstances, nobody ever totally let go of somebody they really loved and lost. The first thing Robert E. had to do was acknowledge that Emily's death had affected him in the first place. He'd managed convincing himself for far too long that he was a man's man and he wasn't going to let any of his feelings show. He had to be strong; for himself, for LB… especially for LB. Ultimately, it was for his son that Robert E. realized he needed to move on too; at least a little bit.

Robert E. dreaded the question long before LB asked it.

"What happened to Mommy? Don't she want to be with us anymore?"

As a widower, Robert E. still had a lot to work through which he largely disregarded. He still had living to do, errands to run and encounters with well-meaning people who still occasionally offered every kind of advice imaginable. He couldn't ignore his son's well-being.

To his face, people commented how he seemed to be handling life after Emily so well. Really? How else was he supposed to be handling it? Behind his back was another story. On more than one occasion after Emily died, he'd walked into a room only to be greeted by awkward silence. He was well aware of what people were thinking and saying. They didn't want to hear how he was doing, not really. They were simply going through the motions, feeling compelled, obligated. In their minds, they thought they already knew. They thought they were being good people, doing their bit in acknowledging him, not dwelling on Emily's death or how Robert E. was now a single parent living back home with his own parents. It was his misfortune, not theirs. Life had gone on for them, but not for Robert E. How else was he supposed to handle losing the love of his life?

The end of that year brought Robert E. to a new place in his life. After the episode at the house, he'd determined that not only for his own sake but for that of his son's that he needed to get on with the business of living. It'd been long enough. He would never forget Emily or the incredible journey they were fortunate to share but he finally decided to get things out, finish the grief-work he was so reluctant to acknowledge and get back to living. He finally made the phone call one Saturday afternoon.

"Hello Max? This is Robert, I mean Bobby Elliott. Jon and Anna's son? Yes, yes sir. We're doing okay. What's that? Oh, I know. Too long." Robert E. had finally decided that he needed to start somewhere. "No sir, not on the phone. There? Sure. I can be there around nine. Yes sir. I'll bring donuts if you have the coffee. See you then."

When Robert E. retired that evening, he fell asleep easily. There was no restlessness, no insomnia and for the first time in years, no heaviness in his heart.

"So that's what sleep feels like." Robert E. glanced at the pillow beside him and saw Emily's picture laying there. With a noticeable ache in his heart, he picked up her photo and held it lovingly in his hands. He thought about all the years, places, and memories they had shared and how he'd handled her loss. He thought long and hard before whispering, "Thank you Emily. We'll never forget you." He kissed her photograph gently and placed the frame on his nightstand.

"Max, Max, Max. I'm trusting in you this morning, man. Don't let me down."

At the breakfast table, Robert E. sat in silence, waiting for his father to come in from finishing chores knowing LB would be following. Despite her sons' quietness, Anna didn't ask any questions. She poured him a cup of coffee and placed it on the table before him. There was a sense of calm to his demeanor this morning, something she hadn't seen in a long time.

"Can I fix you something to eat?" She asked nonchalantly.

Robert E. took a sip of his coffee. "No, Mama. I have an appointment this morning. I'll grab something in town. You mind watching LB for me for a few hours?"

"Do you even have to ask?" Anna was dying to ask her son what his appointment was about but knew he wouldn't reveal any information before he was ready.

Jon and LB came bursting noisily through the front door, their faces red from the cold but laughing as they raced to the kitchen.

"Go on, tell her boy." Jon Elliott took LB's coat and hat and hung them on a peg behind the door before removing his own flannel jacket. "Your daddy's out there, too. Go tell them."

"Guess what? Guess what? The fat beagle got puppies in the barn last night! She isn't fat anymore. She finally got puppies!" LB chattered excitedly.

Anna looked at Jon and sighed. "How many?"

"Six. We've sold all but one. I thought maybe we could find somebody to take that last one off our hands." Jon Elliott directed the question to Robert E. "Maybe somebody's boy needs a pup to pal around with?"

Robert E. had already decided LB could get a puppy and was nodding his head to his father's offer but put a finger to his lips as he pointed at his son. LB was oblivious to the communication going on between his grandfather and daddy and stood by Anna at the stove watching her get ready to cook breakfast.

"Mama. I've got to go. LB, I'll be back in a little while. You keep an eye on Grandma and Grandpa, okay." Robert E. looked at his parents, breathed in the familiar apples and cinnamon scent, and looked out the window. "I'm going up to go talk with Max this morning. I might be a few hours." He looked at his father and said, "It's time. Don't you think?"

Jon Elliott's eyes watered as he quickly nodded his head. "Yep. Let me go move the truck so you can get out."

"But Dad, it's not-"

"Yes it is Bobby." Anna interrupted. "Let your father move the truck so you can get out of the drive." She pointed to LB and dabbed at her own eyes.

Robert E. understood immediately. "You need anything while I'm in town?"

Anna shook her head. "Take all the time you need, son."

Robert E. hugged his mother, hugged his son and disappeared through the door. As he made his way off the porch, his father met him at the steps.

"So you called Max?" Jon asked his son.

Robert E. nodded his head as his father slapped him on the shoulder.

"Good. Good. Take your time, son." Jon Elliott sighed a sigh of relief.

The drive to the church was a familiar one, though one he hadn't made for years. Robert E. was almost amazed that the roof didn't fall in as he stepped through the doors and felt almost relieved when Reverend Max suggested they take their meeting to the parsonage next door.

"I brought donuts." Robert E. smiled as he held the box out to Max.

"And I have a fresh pot of coffee on the burner. Come in, come in. Take a seat."

Robert E. took instant notice of the old, tin coffee pot Max was using. It wasn't even a plug-in percolator like his mothers' ancient coffee maker.

"Max, I swear. You and my mother would work well together. Haven't you ever heard of Mr. Coffee? Black and Decker maybe?" Robert E. nodded his head toward the stove.

"I have one." The reverend pointed a finger to a cart by the door. "I just don't know how to use it. Don't need it."

"Looks like you swiped this one from the set of an old cowboy movie." Robert E. grinned.

"Depression era children. We save everything. I'll bet your mother saves bacon grease and grocery bags, too." Max opened as pantry cupboard revealing wads of plastic bags from the local super-market. "So do I. The bags are actually quite handy to use in the smaller waste-baskets, you know."

Talking to Max felt just like old times. The man never judged, was always ready to offer suggestions and give his own gentle manner of guidance to help his parishioners who presented with spiritual turmoil.

"I don't know where to begin, what to say. I mean, it's not like I've been through this before." Robert E. had gotten past the hardest part; calling Max in the first place."But I've had enough."

"You decided you've had enough." Max reiterated simply. He'd received more than a few calls from Jon and Anna Elliott regarding their son after Emily died. At one point, Jon Elliott voiced a deep concern over his son's gradually acquired habit of drinking and disappearing for entire weekends at a time. Max had been reluctant to confront their son too soon after the death of Emily, confident that Robert would call in his own due time.

"I haven't said anything to Anna but I half expect to get a call from the authorities to come identify his body one of these nights."

"Bet you don't get too many calls like this, eh Rev?" Robert E. joked nervously.

"You would be amazed. I'm just surprised it took you so long to find the courage. I'm glad you finally called. A lot of people have been worrying about you, praying for you. Tell me, what's on your mind Mr. Elliott."

Talking about Emily was easy enough. It was the next part that proved the most difficult for Robert E. Opening up and confessing his thoughts and feelings since Emily died was like admitting what he'd been denying for the past several years. He even detailed the nights he was alone at the house where he thought of finishing off the bottle.

"It's hard to talk about." Robert E. sat back, looking at the man before him. "I know I've needed to do this though. I mean, I haven't been practicing any religion but I still tried talking, you know, to God. I figured a real man shouldn't, wouldn't let those kinds of things bother him." He sipped at his coffee. "I feel like I'm confessing some awful deed."

"You are a real man, but you are also a real human." Max stated simply. "You are allowed to feel emotion. If you didn't, there would be more to worry about."

Robert E. nodded.

"Of course." Max studied Robert E's face, thinking carefully about the words he was going to say next. It had taken the man before him tremendous courage to come talk about something as personal as his grief, to admit that he'd lost his faith, to admit he had almost given up. Max didn't want to sour Robert E's views on religion. He picked up the book on his desk and quickly opened to a marked page.

"With the death of important people in our lives, we make many efforts to understand the meaning and significance of their passing. It has been written that loved ones achieve immortality through their legacy and the accomplishments they leave behind. This makes our memories of those people little packages with big emotion. This is how our loved ones can and should be remembered." Max closed the book and looked at Robert E., peering at him over his glasses. He wasn't preaching, simply talking, and gently encouraging Robert E. to respond from his heart. Not an easy task to accomplish.

Robert E. sat back and inhaled deeply, letting out a slow sigh.

"Max, that was beautiful." Robert E. shook his head.

"It's been a long time Robert Elliott."

"I've got to tell you, Rev. This isn't usually my scene, you know."

"Never is." Max sat back, listening, waiting.

"I mean, what am I supposed to say?"

The pastor looked at Robert with concerned yet gentle eyes. "Ah, this I cannot know, Robert. You called me. What is it that you want to say?" Max sat with his chin resting on his index fingers and smiled his mysterious smile. "Everybody has a story to tell. That's what I'm here for. Let me hear yours."

That day at the parsonage had been an epiphany. Robert E. told Max everything from the day he and Emily first met to all the years they had lost touch and met again. As he spoke and gestured, Robert E. felt an enormous weight lift from his heart. The pain he had been carrying for so long finally started to ease from his mind, at last freeing him from the darkness that had surrounded him since the day he was told Emily was killed.

"Max, I don't know what else to say. I should have come talk to you a long time ago." Robert E. stood to leave.

"One moment Robert." Max unhurriedly turned to search the massive bookcase behind him. "There's something else you need to hear. Bear with me a moment." The pastor reached up and selected a red-covered book from the middle of the shelf. He opened the pages and quickly found the spot he was looking for. "Here." He held the book out to Robert E. "Perhaps you should read this on your own terms."

"Oh, no thanks Rev. I'm good. Really. I'm not the book type anyway." Robert E. thanked Max for his time and stood to leave.

"Not the whole book, my son. Read what's underlined." Max gently insisted.

Robert E. took the book without looking at the title and began to read.

Every Marine who has ever lived is living still- in the Marines who claim the title today. It is that sense of belonging to something that will outlive your own mortality, which gives people a light to live by and a flame to mark their passing…

"Sometimes things happen in our lives for no apparent reason, at least not one known to us at the time. Quite often, as you travel further down the road, the reason becomes clear. You might not like the reason and you don't necessarily have to accept it. But Robert, sometimes that's when your 'a-ha' moment will reveal itself to you. Pay attention. Only you will know when the answer has presented itself."

"Max, thanks again for seeing me. I shouldn't have waited so long." Robert E. didn't know what else to say. "I'd like to borrow this book if you don't mind."

"Of course, of course. Take your time with it."

Though he had been gone all morning, Robert E. still had one more stop to make before returning to his parent's house. After talking with Max, Robert E. suddenly felt different. The heaviness that had been ever present in his heart since the day Emily died felt lighter.

The gates to the cemetery were opened wide. Robert E. chuckled silently to himself, thinking about why anyone felt the need to put a fence around a cemetery in the first place.

"Emily, if I ever needed a sign…" Robert E. knew his destination all too well. "Sure could use a few words from you now, girl." Despite the time that had passed, the grass still had not completely filled in over her grave. Robert E. stood looking at the spot, remembering the scene all too vividly. Dropping to one knee, Robert E. closed his eyes and traced the letters of her name on the cool, copper tablet.

"God Emily, I miss you so much. I'm never going to let him forget you, you know. Not a chance." Robert E. took a deep breath before continuing."I just wanted you to know, I talked with Max today, I mean really talked to him. He started sounding like you used to get; all philosophical and well, I guess that's his job. But he made me think, girl. He really made me think." Robert E. opened his eyes and looked around the cemetery making sure nobody else was within earshot. "I've got to pull my act together. For LB. For you. For me. I'm not letting you go, but I still have to live. I have a life to show and teach to our son. You'd be so proud of him, too. He looks just like you, he acts just like you..." He paused, deep in thought. "So you see, there's no way we can forget you. You've been right here all along. I guess I knew that, but today I really get it. I finally get it Em. I finally got it."

Later that night before he went to bed, Robert E. reached under the bed to touch the red, cedar box, reaching for Emily one more time. He picked up her picture from the bedside table and held it against his heart. This time was different. This time there was a sense of closure. "I'll only be a memory away." This time everything was all right. Where it had been dark for so long, Robert E. finally began to see a light.

It took the two of them a long time on an incredibly crooked road. Remember, theirs was not meant to be a story with any specific lesson to put across or moral to convey. It was simply a story about two people needing to be told. It wasn't a simple one, not one solely about lost love revisited or of strangers passing like ships in the night. Instead it was a story reminding us about a few things in life...things we all share.

Emily's Robert E. wasn't supposed to be a 'feel-good story' with a 'happily ever after' ending. Instead, it was a tale of two people who were connected on some ethereal level whose lives were directly affected by a little war in a country called Iraq and the fact that they ever knew one another at all. It was a story affected by Fate, circumstance, chance, you name it. There's wasn't a love story in the predictable sense of what love stories were usually considered, but one about love; about a love one man never knew he gave, never intended to give up and a woman who always knew. Nobody could have planned this stuff. It just happened.

Prologue

We can change some things in our lives completely.
Other things we can alter to some extent.
There are many things, however, that are irrevocable.

Sybil Leek

The cost of any war is especially great when the statisticians go beyond quoting the obvious operating costs and start including the number of casualties produced on all sides; ours, theirs, civilian and military alike. Casualties aren't just about lives that can never be given back but also about lives seized. When a soldiers' life is taken, who immediately thinks of the widow, widower or orphans that are created? It doesn't matter what side a soldier fights for, the results are the same. People rarely think about those who are left behind or about any impending consequences resulting from a person's death; soldier or otherwise.

We should in the very least acknowledge, if not downright honor the families and friends of individuals who fell while serving their country so unselfishly: the living left behind to pick up the pieces. When a soldier dies, we turn melancholy and thoughtful only for a moment to reflect. We barely think about how many people have witnessed/ experienced the devastation of shattered hopes and future dreams when they spied that government vehicle pull into their driveway. We might think about how many people have been roused from comfortable slumber in the early morning hours who answered an unanticipated phone call or were awakened by an unexpected knock upon their door and we are always glad it wasn't us.

"Fair winds and following seas…"

THE END

Would you like to see your manuscript become a book?

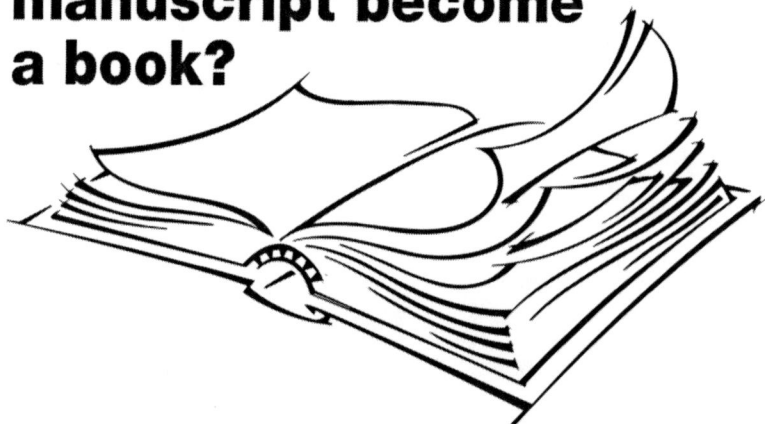

If you are interested in becoming a PublishAmerica author, please submit your manuscript for possible publication to us at:

acquisitions@publishamerica.com

You may also mail in your manuscript to:

**PublishAmerica
PO Box 151
Frederick, MD 21705**

www.publishamerica.com

PublishAmerica

CPSIA information can be obtained at www.ICGtesting.com
Printed in the USA
237746LV00001B/23/P

9 781462 608829